JENNIFER

JENNIFER

The unofficial and unauthorised biography of
JENNIFER LOPEZ
by Marissa Charles

Published by
Kandour Ltd
1-3 Colebrook Place
London N1 8HZ

This edition printed in 2004 for
Bookmart Limited
Registered Number 2372865
Trading as Bookmart Ltd
Blaby Road
Wigston
Leicester LE18 4SE

First published June 2004

ISBN 1–904756–07–7

Production services:
Metro Media Ltd

Author: Marissa Charles

With thanks to: Jenny Ross, Emma Hayley,
Lee Coventry, Helena L, Paula Field

Cover design: Mike Lomax
Cover Image: Rex Features

Inside Images: Rex Features

© Kandour Ltd

Printed and bound by Nørhaven Paperback, Denmark

FOREWORD

This series of biographies is a celebration of celebrity. It features some of the world's greatest modern-day icons including movie stars, soap personalities, pop idols, comedians and sporting heroes. Each biography examines their struggles, their family background, their rise to stardom and in some cases their struggle to stay there. The books aim to shed some light on what makes a star. Why do some people succeed when others fail?

Written in a light-hearted and lively way, and coupled with the most up-to-date details on the world's favourite heroes and heroines, this series is an entertaining read for anyone interested in the world of celebrity. Discover all about their career highlights – what was the defining moment to propel them into superstardom? No story about fame is without its ups and downs. We reveal the emotional rollercoaster ride that many of these stars have been on to stay at the top. Read all about your most adored personalities in these riveting books.

JENNIFER LOPEZ

CONTENTS

JENNIFER LOPEZ

FACT FILE

Full name: Jennifer Lynn Lopez
Date of birth: 24 July 1970
Place of birth: The Bronx, New York, USA
Eye colour: Brown
Height: 5' 6"
Marriages: Ojani Noa (1997 – 1998);
Cris Judd (2001 – 2003)
Boyfriends: David Cruz (1985 – 1996);
Sean 'Puff Daddy' Combs (1999 – 2001);
Ben Affleck (2002 – 2004)
Children: None
Parents: Guadalupe and David Lopez
Siblings: Leslie and Lynda

Star sign: Leo (23 July – 22 August)
Leos, the lions of the zodiac, are characterised by their pride, generosity and outgoing behaviour. Fiercely independent, they are driven by a desire to excel at whatever occupation they set their minds to. Forever ambitious, they aim to be the centre of attention in their career of choice. Leos also tend to be stubborn and assertive but as friends they are open-hearted and loyal. Never modest, they are people who will not be ignored.

JENNIFER LOPEZ

FACT FILE

Chinese birth sign: Dog

Those born in the year of the Dog are loyal individuals who are faithful to their friends. They are people who are blessed with a strong code of ethics and, as a result, in their professional and personal lives, set a high standard for themselves and others. Although they can be moody at times they are happiest when engaged in an activity. They also have a good business sense.

Career high:

In 2001 Jennifer Lopez became the first female artist to have a number one movie, *The Wedding Planner,* and a chart-topping hit, *Love Don't Cost a Thing*, in America at the same time.

1

Introduction

INTRODUCTION

Had she been anyone else the headlines would have read 'Grandmother hits the jackpot' or 'Retired teacher strikes it rich.' The story would have garnered interest in her home state, maybe the neighbouring one, but beyond that region one woman's $2.4 million booty in Atlantic City would hardly have commanded the attention of the American nation. In a country where a roll-over lottery fund could equal $50 million or more the win was good for her but not worth holding the front pages of regional newspapers across the land.

This winner, however, was someone special. In April 2004 her luck in Atlantic City (the

INTRODUCTION

gambling seaside town and New Jersey's mini-Las Vegas) found its way into newspapers, not just throughout the United States, but abroad as well. For this lady was the mother of someone whose name, even when abbreviated, commands attention. The retired kindergarten teacher, who hit the jackpot that month, was Guadalupe – the mother of Jennifer Lopez.

When you are a celebrity it seems that even those closest to you can send the world's media into a state of frenzy. And when you are the artist-also-known-as-J-Lo – actress, dancer, singer, songwriter, entrepreneur – and you were almost married to a major Hollywood star it doesn't take much to get the pens of celebrity columnists twitching. A walk to the grocery store is enough to trigger an avalanche of paparazzi, much less the unexpected fortune of your own mother.

For Jennifer Lopez it was another slice from an already extraordinary life. But if anyone thought that the Lopez clan were the luckiest family on the planet, they were sadly mistaken. Yes Guadalupe may be the mother of one of the most beautiful women in the world, an actress who has shared the screen with the likes of Jack Nicholson, Michael Caine and George Clooney, who

INTRODUCTION

has her own line of clothes, her own restaurant and does all this (and more) alongside a successful singing career. But Guadalupe's daughter is also a woman who had to fight for her fame and wealth every step of the way. Her journey demanded she hold fast to a vision that for many years she alone could see. It meant sacrificing relationships, moving to the other side of the country and giving up on a promising academic career plus a life of security.

When Guadalupe's daughter told her parents she was going to be a performer, back in the Eighties, it was like telling them she was going to Atlantic City in the hope that, if she picked one machine out of a collection of thousands, she would select the one that would make her a millionaire. The story of Jennifer Lopez is the story of a woman who did everything in her power to find that one machine, and she would not rest until she located it. She would either hit that jackpot or die trying, but she was going nowhere until she had become a millionaire.

In this instance being a 'millionaire' meant becoming one of the most recognisable faces on the planet; to be part of that select group of people whose lives are immortalised on the big screen. In 2004 music and fashion have unfortunately rooted

JENNIFER LOPEZ

INTRODUCTION

the image of Jennifer Lopez in a particular place and time. Her songs (with their Latin roots and R&B beats), her sense of style (Versace with a bling-bling trim), her background (set in the Bronx) are like magnets to the words 'ghetto fabulous', 'hip-hop' and 'urban'. But, upon closer inspection, her story is no different to that of the stars of old whose drive and passion compelled them to entertain, to express themselves be it through drama, song or dance. Like a Sammy Davis Junior, a Marilyn Monroe or a Judy Garland, Jennifer Lopez could never be anything else other than who she has become. It was what she was put on this earth to do.

Viewed from this vantage point it seems that, just as luck had nothing to do with her success, neither did choice. The success of Guadalupe's daughter was not dependent on the spin of a roulette wheel or the tossing of dice. It was, quite simply, meant to be.

2

27 December 1999

JENNIFER LOPEZ

27 DECEMBER 1999

I t is a Sunday night in New York City when a young couple decide to hit town. December 1999 is nearly over and the holiday season is reaching its climax as people across the globe anticipate one of the biggest party nights of all time. From London to Sydney, Paris to New York, millions around the world are preparing to welcome the new millennium. On the eve of the 21st century everyone wants to make Prince's prophetic words come true and party like it's 1999.

The young couple who are enjoying the delights of the city have every reason to celebrate. Jennifer Lopez and her beau, Sean 'Puff Daddy'

JENNIFER LOPEZ

Combs are perfect ambassadors for New York. Symbolically they represent everything the city is famous for. She, the Latin beauty from the Bronx, and he, the celebrated record producer, rapper and entrepreneur from Harlem, are as New York as baseball and hot dogs, Frank Sinatra's signature tune and the Manhattan skyline all rolled into one. Independently they are the American dream personified – the boy and girl from next door who clawed their way to the top. Together they are brash, cocky and ostentatious – the ghetto-fabulous version of Richard Burton and Elizabeth Taylor, whose wealth adorns their fingers, ears and shoulders in an array of diamonds, furs and haute couture. Jennifer and Puff fascinate the men and women of the press – both separately and together. Reams of paper have been dedicated to the couple's relationship. Will they or won't they make it down the aisle? And the MTV generation have catapulted them to the top of the music tree, furnishing their lavish lifestyle along the way.

Their success is justified. Before the phrase 'bling-bling' tripped off every Fleet Street journalist's tongue Puff Daddy was trailing a blaze in hip-hop, weaving catchy hooks and phat beats that would help the genre to make an assault on the

JENNIFER LOPEZ

mainstream charts well into the mid-Noughties. The young music mogul started his career at the urban label, Uptown Records on the cusp of the Nineties. As an intern, and then as an A&R executive, he made his name by working with artists such as the vocal group Jodeci – an edgy quartet that rivalled Boys 2 Men – and the queen of hip-hop soul, Mary J Blige. By 1999 29-year-old Puff was the chief executive of his own label, Bad Boy Records. He had worked with everyone from Mariah Carey and Madonna to his friend, the murdered rapper, the Notorious BIG. Now a successful recording artist in his own right, he owned a chain of soul-food restaurants, a clothing line called Sean John, a Park Avenue house and a place in the Hamptons, which the American domestic goddess herself, Martha Stewart, was said to have decorated.

It was at this house that Puff and his girlfriend, the dancer-turned-actress-turned-singer Jennifer Lopez, were staying on 27 December 1999. Jennifer had come to the public's attention earlier in the decade as one of the Fly Girls – a funky, female dance troupe who featured on the television comedy show, *In Living Color*. She had since become an actress, winning critical acclaim in the movies *Out of Sight* and *Selena*. In 1999 she ventured into music, riding on the Latin wave, promising to become the new millennium's answer to Eighties' pop sensation Gloria Estefan. Jennifer had already scored a number one hit in America with her debut single If You Had My Love, taken from her first album *On the 6*. Now she was taking a long-deserved break with Puff before she continued to promote her music well into the new year.

On the surface all seemed to be well. Earlier that day Puff called the manager at a popular Times Square hotspot – Club New York. He booked a table for Jennifer, his 'crew' and himself. There was no suggestion that anything untoward was going to happen. New York was their city. This was their time and they were going to do what young urbanites around the world would also be doing that very night – enjoy themselves. Christmas 1999 was one long party that was a hair's breadth away from its end. And, though they weren't to know it, so was Puff and Jennifer's relationship.

Exactly what happened during the few hours that the couple and their entourage were in the club is unclear. By all accounts the celebrity party were seated in a VIP section. The champagne flowed freely and there was no hint of trouble until Puff, Jennifer and co' decided to leave. Witnesses say that as Puffy was on his way out, a young man threw a fistful of dollars at him. The details of what happened next would be poured over by prosecutors, defence attorneys, reporters and New York society for months to come.

What *is* known is that shots were fired and during the fracas three people — two men and a woman — were injured. The woman had been shot in the face and both men received minor shoulder injuries.

It was 2.20am and within minutes of the shootings Puff, Jennifer and two of their associates left the club. Police statements released the next morning said the couple were stopped in a speeding car 10 minutes after the incident took place. The celebrity duo was not immediately recognised by the police officer on the scene. Jennifer and Puff sat in the backseat of his Jeep. In the front sat their driver, Wardel Fenderson, and a bodyguard, Anthony Jones. Most importantly, a loaded 9mm handgun was found in the vehicle. It was not registered in the name of any of the occupants.

Later that morning the news would be blasted

27 DECEMBER 1999

on television screens worldwide. The headlines were too delicious to ignore. Actress and singer Jennifer Lopez and her boyfriend Puff Daddy had been arrested. Jennifer would be exonerated within 24 hours, released without charge "based on the evaluation of the evidence" police spokesman Wayne Brison said later. Puff and his associates were not so lucky. Fenderson and Jones would both be charged with criminal possession of a weapon and stolen property. (The gun was registered as stolen in Georgia.) Puff, who was released on $10,000 bail, would face the same charges.

The next day, as New York sizzled with details of the previous night's events, the rapper and producer held a press conference. He took the opportunity to profess his innocence. He insisted that he had nothing to do with the incident, that he didn't own a gun and that he was definitely not in possession of one on that night.

It was not until 16 March 2001 that a jury found Puff innocent of all charges. By that time the young man was chastened by the incident. Flanked by his mother and his attorney Johnnie Cochran, who had successfully defended OJ Simpson five years before, he told the waiting press "I give all glory to God."

JENNIFER LOPEZ

Absent from his side was the woman who had been with him on the night of the shooting. Only a month earlier, on Valentine's Day, before the trial came to court, Puff announced that he and Jennifer Lopez were no more. A few months later she would be engaged to Cris Judd, an unknown dancer who appeared in the video for her single *Love Don't Cost a Thing*. She had moved on.

Both Puff and Jennifer re-emerged from the ordeal, phoenix-like. Both adopted new names. Sean Combs re-christened himself P Diddy. Jennifer took up the nickname given to her by fans, J-Lo – the title of her second album.

Most significantly the actress and singer left the events of 27 December behind her without sullying her reputation. Personally she remained loyal and stood by her man for over a year. Professionally she never broke her stride. Before the incident critics could claim Jennifer was riding on her boyfriend's musical coat tails. After it, and without him, they could not deny the success of her two follow-up albums. Before the shootings they could dismiss her as decorative fluff, an opportunist who amounted to little more than a pretty face. When she became the first female artist to top the American singles chart and have a number one hit movie (*The Wedding Planner*) at the same time, those comments quietened.

Jennifer's love life, however, would continue to titillate gossip columnists around the world long after her union with Puff had ended. But what the events of 27 December 1999 and its aftermath demonstrated was that Jennifer Lopez had arrived. If she were not a global superstar before the shooting, she would rarely be out of the headlines after it. Most importantly, it proved that through focus, determination and hard work she could overcome any scandal that might come her way. Those traits had served her well in the past and, as she faced the world without Puff, they would not fail her now.

3

The Bronx

JENNIFER LOPEZ

THE BRONX

There must be something in the water. Or maybe the earth in that part of New York is especially fertile. Maybe they grow them that way over there. How else can you explain it?

Cast your eye down the list of famous people who were either born, raised or have lived in the Bronx and it reads like an American edition of *Who's Who*. Each one has emerged from that area a bona fide star. In fact 'star' is a trite way to describe some of them. Anne Bancroft and Tony Curtis are more than mere stars they are Hollywood legends. Billy Joel is not just a musician but an accomplished singer-songwriter

THE BRONX

who has made an invaluable contribution to the soundtrack of American life. What about Calvin Klein and Ralph Lauren – are they simply dressmakers? What of Stanley Kubrick, Edgar Allen Poe and Colin Powell – for these individuals the word 'star' is an insult, an understatement, an underestimation of their huge talent. They were and are so much more than that.

The roll call of famous Bronxites is so impressive that if you had to pick a place on the planet that would spawn Jennifer Lopez you would choose that borough, in that city, at that time in the United States.

There is much about the character of the Bronx that connects it to its famous daughter. The name alone contrives an image that is tough and hardwearing. It symbolises an area that is peopled by individuals who are unwilling to be swayed from or denied their dreams. The word 'Bronx' sounds urban – something about it smacks of the metropolis. It has that industrial feel as though the people who live there put their shoulders to a giant wheel that grinds until something miraculous happens.

Like all of America the history of the Bronx is one of migration. It was a Swedish sea captain who lived in The Netherlands, who was to give the

THE BRONX

Bronx its name. In 1639 Jonas Bronck became the borough's first settler when he bought 500 acres of land that became known as 'Broncksland'. Over time other immigrants would come to the area and make it their own. Severe famine in Ireland in the early nineteenth century led to the arrival of thousands of Irish labourers and by the middle of the 1800s an American economic boom attracted a wave of Germans. And so the ebb and flow of migration continued until it produced the 'melting pot' that we know today. The Bronx is a patchwork of colour and culture with Russians, Jamaicans, Cubans, Pakistanis, Vietnamese and Greeks all contributing to its society.

A sizeable proportion of that population is Puerto Rican. Though their share of the borough's community is falling the American census of 2000 revealed that the two largest Puerto Rican strongholds in the United States are Brooklyn and the Bronx. In 1990 the Puerto Ricans accounted for more than a quarter of the latter's population and 20 years prior to that, due to the community's great migration of the Fifties and Sixties, 20 per cent of residents had roots in the Caribbean island. It was in that year, 1970, on 24 July, that Jennifer Lynn Lopez was born.

JENNIFER LOPEZ

THE BRONX

David and Guadalupe were already the proud parents of one daughter when they had their second child. Jennifer joined her older sister Leslie in the Lopez household in the summer of 1970. A few years later the family would be complete when the third and last daughter, Lynda, was born. David and Guadalupe raised their children on Blackrock Avenue in Castle Hill, the south Bronx. It was a typical middle-class existence in a typical middle-class neighbourhood. David, a computer technician, and Guadalupe, a kindergarten teacher, raised the girls on the twin principles of religion and hard work. The Roman Catholic faith and school were two non-negotiable fixtures in the Lopez home. Both, Jennifer's parents believed, would supply the girls with discipline. Education in particular would be their route to a successful life and it was impressed upon them to do well in school.

Like most immigrants raising first-generation Americans David and Guadalupe never forgot the values ingrained in them in the land of their birth. Although they were both born in Puerto Rico they made the permanent move to the States when they were children. As adults and as parents their roots to their homeland remained unbroken. Safely ensconced in the Bronx where the Puerto Rican

THE BRONX

population was significant and growing they could raise their girls in an environment where the influence of their community and culture was strong.

Because a sound education was so highly valued in the Lopez household Jennifer, Leslie and Lynda were encouraged to work hard at school. Caribbean parents, wherever in the world they are located be it America, Britain, Canada or home on the islands, prize highly a good education. No matter how poor you are or what section of society you come from the goal in life is to get that piece of paper that will secure your future. In the Lopez home education was cherished even more because Guadalupe was a teacher.

Childhood friends of Jennifer remember that her parents were strict and insisted that, whatever else was going on in her life, her schoolwork came first. The principles of religion and education were united when David and Guadalupe sent their daughter to Holy Family, a Catholic elementary school. From there she progressed to Preston High, a private school for young women that re-emphasised the twin values of Christian faith and academic diligence.

Friends and former teachers say that the young Jennifer needed no encouragement in that department. When it came to schoolwork she was naturally gifted. Hard work and perseverance ensured that she got good grades.

Jennifer Lopez was not just a good pupil; she was what all university admissions tutors say they long for – a rounded student. The stamina she displays in her music videos today hark back to the extracurricular activities she took up when she was at school. Jennifer was on the track and softball teams and also attended dance classes once the academic day was over. Inside the walls of Preston High, she demonstrated an interest in theatre. She was a member of the drama club and a home video of her singing *Day by Day* in a production of *Godspell* periodically surfaces in many a documentary about her life.

The fact that Jennifer was not a dull, one-dimensional child can also be attributed to the efforts of her parents. If religion and education are two values held dear by Puerto Rican families they are rested on the foundation of a third – culture, especially the Caribbean and Latino culture. Jennifer's parents may have instilled in her the value of hard work, but they also encouraged a love of music. By her own admission music was something that she gravitated to.

JENNIFER LOPEZ

THE BRONX

And who could blame her. Step back into the Seventies for a minute and recall the sounds of that era that would have influenced Jennifer and her peers. It was the age of disco, of the Bee Gees, The Jacksons, John Travolta strutting his stuff in *Saturday Night Fever*, Abba, Donna Summer and celebrities indulging in the hedonism that was Studio 54. Fast-forward to the Eighties and you encounter a different type of performer, people like Madonna, Prince, Michael Jackson and his sister Janet (who Jennifer would later work with) did not just get up on stage and sing their songs into a microphone. Instead they presented their music like mini musicals and whether they were in an auditorium or on MTV they gave their audience the whole package in flamboyant style – with dancers, multiple costume changes, big hair and loud make-up.

Jennifer was exposed to these musical trends and would have witnessed firsthand another one that was conceived and nurtured on her doorstep – hip-hop. Back then it was called rap and the lyrics and beats of Run DMC, Slick Rick and LL Cool J (another future Lopez collaborator) didn't just affect what black and Hispanic youth listened to, it had an impact on the way they dressed and danced. The latest sportswear and jewellery were desirable and a new funkier, edgier way of movement found its way from break-dancing street bouts into music videos, films and television shows.

But the middle daughter of David and Guadalupe was not inspired by the latest trends alone. At home she would have been fed a diet laden with the sounds of Puerto Rico. The African-Caribbean rhythms of salsa and merengue would never have been far away. One of Jennifer's favourite musicals at this time was *West Side Story*, which focused on and, in many ways, celebrated her Puerto Rican heritage.

Embodied in this little girl was a multitude of sounds, all jostling for attention, all vying for first place. From the age of five Jennifer was able to release them at the singing and dance classes that she attended. But for the little girl from the Bronx dancing was not meant to be a hobby, an adjunct to her daily life. It was an overwhelming passion that would place her at odds with the desires of her family. Despite the pleas of her parents, while her academic achievement could and did take Jennifer to college, it was her ability to move that paved her way to the successful life they always wanted her

THE BRONX

to have. Her feet were her 'piece of paper', her ticket that would help her to dance her way right out of the Bronx. Like those who went before her Jennifer Lopez would use her talent to secure her place in entertainment history. Before she could do that though she had to convince the two people who loved her the most and who wanted the best for her – her parents.

4

Crossroads

JENNIFER LOPEZ

CROSSROADS

A t a glance their stories seem quite different. They were born 12 years apart – one in Bay City, Michigan, the other in the Bronx, New York. The older woman came from a big family – she was the third of six children. The younger one was the middle child of three. Their identities could also be divided along racial lines. One woman is of mixed heritage – French-Canadian and Italian – the other sits under the umbrella entitled Hispanic. One lost her mother when she was still a child and believes that this loss could have contributed to her hunger for success. The maternal guidance offered to the other throughout

CROSSROADS

her childhood resulted in her determination to make something of herself.

The two women described above are both familiar to us. The older woman born to a large family in Michigan is Madonna. The younger Hispanic female born in the Bronx 12 years later is the subject of this book, Jennifer Lopez. Despite obvious differences there are many similarities in these two women's stories. Both were raised in strict Roman Catholic families and were taught the importance of hard work. Although they would make their names in the entertainment industry both Madonna and Jennifer were good students who, according to classmates, were independent and strong-minded. Even in their school days they had no truck with what other people thought of them. But nothing unites these women more than the unique role dance played in their lives. It gave them momentum, a platform and opened the doors to so much more in their lives.

Both Madonna and Jennifer Lopez had the ability, and opportunity, to go to college. In fact both of them indulged in higher education for a short period of time. Madonna studied dance at the University of Michigan for a year and a half, while Jennifer began a business studies course at

CROSSROADS

Baruch University but did not graduate. Both of them were pulled away from the lure of education by the thrill of the dance world. The two women frustrated their parents by their determination to live the chaotic, unpredictable life of an artist. Both shunned the security of their homes and thrust themselves into the bosom of the city of New York when they were still only teenagers.

Nearly 30 years later Madonna's story is now the stuff of legend. In July 1978 the 19-year-old arrived in New York with $35 to her name and a bag full of dreams. The location was Times Square. A decade later, Jennifer Lopez would strike a blow for her independence in a similar fashion. Although there was no need for a cab – the heart of New York City was a comparative stone's throw away – and the story reads less like a fairytale, the central theme remains the same. An academically gifted young college girl shuns a life of stability and pins her hopes on becoming a dancer, while her parents wait at home. Which young woman who has watched *Fame* or *Flashdance* hasn't dreamed it would happen to her? That some day, somebody would notice them, recognise their talent, and lift them out of their mundane, ordinary lives? Fortunately for Madonna and Jennifer that was the case, but they were instrumental in making it happen. Opportunity didn't come looking for them, they threw themselves in its path. They didn't wait for the phone to ring. They bypassed the phone, packed their bags and went in search of their dreams.

When Jennifer graduated from Preston High School in 1987 the notion that she would become a professional dancer was just that – an idea. It was by no means her reality. Her everyday life was far different. When she was not studying a business course at Baruch University at the City University of New York she was performing secretarial duties at a local attorney's office.

The lawyer in question was Thomas J Lavin who was based in the Bronx. Thomas can still remember Jennifer who, even then, stood out as a bright teenager with potential. However it was not her prowess as a dancer that commanded his attention but the sharpness of her mind. Her ability to catch on to the task at hand meant that her role expanded from a secretarial one to include paralegal duties. At the age of 18 Jennifer was preparing summons and complaints.

The dedication she displayed at the attorney's office she applied in equal measure to her studies. One friend, who also went to school

CROSSROADS

with Jennifer, recalls the two of them memorising their work on the train on their way to college.

So far, so normal. A young girl goes to university and supplements her income with a part-time job. But Jennifer wanted more. After spotting a newspaper advert offering a scholarship to study dance at a prestigious studio she took the plunge and decided to attend the auditions. As opportunities go this one was ripe for the picking.

The audition was to study at the Phil Black Studio in Manhattan. Phil Black was, and is, a renowned dance instructor who has worked with such luminaries as John Travolta and Madonna. His success rate among his students was impressive. The proportion of them that made it into show business was once reported to exceed 70 per cent. Here was a man whose passion for dance infused every bone in his body. When he was not developing his craft, he was competing. When he was not teaching classes he was performing on Broadway. In recent years even old age and illness have not detracted him from his first love. He continues to teach at the Broadway Dance Center in New York.

But in the late Eighties Phil Black ran an outfit under his name. When Jennifer Lopez turned up she impressed his team with her ability to keep up with all the moves the choreographer could throw at her. She was not a professional dancer, but she had something – a spark, a desire to do well, an ability to take instruction yet put her own spin on things. Des Calderon, Phil's business partner, can remember the day she walked into the building. The moves that singled her out on the dance floor were accompanied by an attitude that confirmed her determination to succeed should she win the scholarship. As Calderon later told VH1, he asked each performer to explain in writing why they should be accepted onto the course. Jennifer's response revealed that the values her parents instilled in her were not wasted.

When asked to describe herself the teenager wrote that she was "ambitious, hard working and dedicated". She was also, she insisted, responsible. By the time she was 20 or 21, she declared, she *would* be dancing professionally. "That," she wrote, "is what I see myself doing." Her ability to clearly map out her vision of the future can be traced back to childhood lessons. But this time perhaps she took her cue from the Catholic Church. Faith, the Bible teaches in Hebrews 11:1 is the substance of things hoped for, the evidence of things not seen. Most teenagers could only 'hope'

CROSSROADS

for the picture Jennifer painted for herself. Jennifer had faith and was accepted at the Phil Black Studio.

To fellow students and staff the woman who would become known around the world as J-Lo was an ambitious and dedicated pupil. She worked hard, responded with commitment and was rewarded for her efforts. Like most teachers thrilled by a gifted student's ability to learn, Calderon had a soft spot for Jennifer. Over the next few months he worked with her and urged her to recognise her special talent.

Calderon played an instrumental role in the early career of Jennifer Lopez because he helped to tip the balance. Never one to do anything by half Jennifer was attempting to juggle three commitments and for once was failing to excel at all the tasks she had taken on. It quickly dawned on her that she could not be all things to all people – a business undergraduate, a part-time paralegal and a dancer. Something had to give. She had to make a choice and someone was going to be disappointed. According to Calderon it was he who advised her to recognise her gift for dancing, follow her dream and drop out of university. And that is exactly what she did.

CROSSROADS

Needless to say Jennifer's parents were upset by the decision she had made. Throughout her life they had ingrained in her the value of education and the need to get that piece of paper that would be her passport in life. Now she was throwing it away to pursue a childhood dream. Aged 18 she did more than just drop out of Baruch University, she left the Lopez family home for good. The headstrong teenager turned her back on a college education, left Castle Hill and moved in with a friend in the City.

For better or worse, she had made her decision. And like Madonna Ciccone a decade before she turned her back on a life of stability and put her face to the uncertain winds of New York determined that, come what may, she would be a dancer.

5

I want to be a dancer

JENNIFER LOPEZ

I WANT TO BE A DANCER

The year is 1988 and the world does not know it yet but it is about to change. On the surface it is business as usual. Babies are born – in Britain the Duke and Duchess of York celebrate the birth of their first child, Princess Beatrice. New drugs go on the market – Prozac, a small pill that promises to make a big impact on the war against depression, makes its debut. Books are written – Salman Rushdie ignites the fury of Iran's Ayatollah Khomeini with the publication of his controversial novel, *The Satanic Verses*. And presidents are elected – the Republicans extend their reign at the White

JENNIFER LOPEZ

I WANT TO BE A DANCER

House by four years when Ronald Reagan's second in command, George Bush (the father, not the son), is elected America's leader.

But for all the global events that took place in 1988 one small occurrence went unreported. An 18-year-old young woman left her childhood home in the Bronx, turned her back on a college education and set her mind to become a professional dancer. It may have been a major turning point in the Lopez household, but for the outside world at that time it was as minuscule as an ant batting its eyelid. It was non-existent. This event was not going to steal column inches from George Bush, the president-elect. Neither would it knock Princess Beatrice's photograph off the front page of Fleet Street's tabloids. Nevertheless the determination of Jennifer Lopez to become a dancer was significant and it would have a global impact.

Why was the action of this determined teen so significant? It was significant because in 1988 it was a long shot. Back then, during the last hurrah of the Eighties, Latin-American culture was not basking in the mainstream spotlight it would hold in the late Nineties. It was a full decade before Ricky Martin would be *Living La Vida Loca* at the top of the Billboard charts and

I WANT TO BE A DANCER

any successes that Latinos had were individual ones not part of a collective movement. Cuban-American Gloria Estefan was one exception and by 1988 songs such as *1-2-3* and *Bad Boy* had made her a household name. Respected group Los Lobos did their bit to carry the flame and in 1987 introduced Ritchie Valens' *La Bamba* – the title track from the film of the same name – to a new generation of music listeners.

But, despite these individual successes, there was no Latin-American equivalent of Hitsville, USA. There was no Motown that the public could look to, that boasted a stable of recognisable names that would trip instantly off the tongue of every person from Tokyo to Timbuktu.

For Hispanics other stars did exist but they were the musicians they listened to, en masse, within their communities; artists they admired who garnered huge respect and adulation without capturing either the attention or the imagination of the mainstream press. This trend was and is replicated throughout other communities sitting on the edge of the Western ideal. Indians had Bollywood long before Andrew Lloyd-Webber brought that genre to the stages of the West End and Broadway. Jamaicans enjoyed dancehall

I WANT TO BE A DANCER

before either Blu Cantrell or Beyoncé featured the lyrical ability of Sean Paul on their hit records. And the Trinidadian thirst for calypso and soca thrives whether or not one of their own makes an impact on the British or American pop charts.

And so it was with the Latin-American community in 1988. Today every recording artist and actor wears his or her Hispanic credentials with pride. Back then there was no Christina Aguilera, Christina Milian or Cameron Diaz in the popular consciousness. And the only Iglesias that women lusted over was Julio, not his 13-year-old son Enrique.

On-screen Latinos shared the same complaint of African-Americans and black people in Britain. In the cinema and on television Hispanics were largely pigeonholed into undesirable roles if they made an appearance at all. In gritty urban dramas they would be the troubled teen, the drug dealer or street hustler. Positive role models were few and far between. Jimmy Smits, who played Victor Sifuentes in the hit legal drama *LA Law*, was the notable exception.

In 1988 there was no Salma Hayek or Penelope Cruz for us to applaud, whose beauty women could celebrate and men could lust over.

JENNIFER LOPEZ

I WANT TO BE A DANCER

Benicio Del Toro, who had appeared in *Miami Vice* the year before, was a long way away from receiving an Academy Award. Today the 'show' business is much more receptive to Latinos. Discrimination still exists but many of the barriers have come down. In 1988 the world had a different landscape and the road that Jennifer Lopez was about to negotiate seemed riddled with potholes. Had she told her family that she was going to the moon, rather than Manhattan to become a dancer, it would seem more in the realm of possibility.

Jennifer admitted this herself in an interview with *Eonline*. On her family's thoughts about her entrance into the entertainment business she explained that Latinos didn't do that sort of thing. To her parents, family and friends it was a crazy, foolish idea – a spin on the roulette wheel that you're more likely to lose than win.

At first the odds were stacked against Jennifer and like any young person entering the industry she went on an endless round of auditions only to be knocked back time and again. Her mentor and teacher at the Phil Black Studio, Des Calderon, helped her out whenever he could. He put together dance troupes that would perform in the city's

I WANT TO BE A DANCER

nightspots including The Roxy and The Cat Club, ensuring there was always a place for Jennifer.

The jobs would be an additional early training ground. On those small stages, long before she would perform before sell-out crowds, she learnt how to command the attention of an audience. At those clubs she honed her craft and focussed on her ultimate goal.

Some old footage from *Yo! MTV Raps* – a popular hip-hop show on the cable music channel – demonstrates Jennifer's early ability to grab attention and hold on to it. It is March 1989 and the presenter, Fab 5 Freddy, is introducing the world to a new hip-hop artist, MC Hammer. The producers of the show chose to shoot that particular episode at the Phil Black Studio with dancers in the background. Jennifer was among those selected to appear, contributing to the high-energy atmosphere that would come to characterise MC Hammer as a performer. It is in these shots – Jennifer's first television appearance – that we witness her ability to draw the viewer in. As Fab 5 Freddy talks to the audience at home, the camera spans the gathering of dancers behind him. A young Jennifer Lopez, her face framed with dark ringlets, stands out from the crowd. As

I WANT TO BE A DANCER

she tosses her head and moves her body, jutting and strutting with attitude, she oozes confidence. It is a small achievement and an even smaller television appearance but it seems that Jennifer is going to enjoy this moment no matter how brief it is. She moves in front of the camera as if she belongs there, at times looks into it and holds its gaze and it isn't even her show.

Jennifer got a better opportunity to shine soon after when she won a place on a performance troupe that was about to go on a tour of Europe. It was the *Golden Musicals of Broadway* revue tour and, for Jennifer, it was her first proper dancing job.

On paper it may sound exotic – a wonderful opportunity for a young girl from the Bronx to tour Europe and see another part of the world. In reality the tour was demanding and the woman who would later be accused of being a diva, would travel in between shows on an uncomfortable bus for four to eight hours at a time. Yet work colleagues recall that the tough New Yorker faced the difficulties head on and spoke up whenever she deemed the conditions to be unacceptable. Even then it is said that Jennifer Lopez had an almost unshakeable self-belief in her abilities. Although it was the start of her career as a performer she

I WANT TO BE A DANCER

showed signs of wanting to be more than a dancer. She wanted to sing. A personal highlight of the tour was the rare opportunity she had to play the part of Anita in an excerpt from *West Side Story* – a musical that had been a favourite of hers since her childhood back in the Bronx.

For all her bravado even Jennifer's well-rooted self-belief received the occasional knock. Once, when she was on the road, she rang her mother in tears, upset that she had been overlooked and, unlike the other performers, would not sing a solo set in the show. (Her part as Anita was the exception, not the rule.) Guadalupe's response was not the one her daughter expected. Jennifer was not offered sympathy, a shoulder to cry on, or soothing words. Again her mother taught her a valuable lesson – toughen up. The entertainment business was the path she had chosen and she had better build a robust exterior to cope with it. Jennifer says her mother told her never to call her in tears again.

The lesson was learned and back in America Jennifer returned to the life of a jobbing dancer. Always on the look out for her big break she resumed the round of auditions waiting for that defining moment that would send her on her way.

I WANT TO BE A DANCER

All along she knew that hard work and a tough exterior alone would not pave her way to superstardom. A healthy dose of luck was also needed. To use a hackneyed phrase, she had to be in the right place at the right time. But for Jennifer, the girl who always did her best to be the best, her big break came not when she came first in an audition, but when she came second. For the first time in her career the gamble paid off and her crazy idea didn't seem so crazy after all.

In 1991 Jennifer was not going to the moon but she was going to a place that, in relation to the Bronx, could almost be as far away. She was going to Los Angeles to realise her dream. And not only was she going to become a dancer. She was going to become one of the most recognisable dancers in the country. Jennifer Lopez was going to be a Fly Girl.

6

Making it in LA

JENNIFER LOPEZ

MAKING IT IN LA

There was no other show on television like it. In 1990 a new type of comedy programme burst on to America's Fox network. It was a sketch show but with a difference. The new ratings contender approached subjects other programmes either could not or would not touch. Characters like Homey D Clown – a convict reluctantly working as a clown to fulfil his parole agreement – were welcomed into the living rooms of thousands of Americans. Suddenly skits entitled "Ridin' Miss Daisy" and "Do-It-Yourself Milli Vanilli Kit" became essential viewing. Described by *Variety* magazine as "daring and funny", Fox's

MAKING IT IN LA

new baby appealed to a whole new audience – a generation of people raised on a diet of daytime talk shows and MTV.

The show's greatest strength was its most obvious difference. The clue was in the title – *In Living Color*. This was not a programme with mostly white faces and the obligatory African-American sticking out like a filling in a row of otherwise healthy teeth. This was largely a black production where people of colour had a creative input both in front of and behind the camera. The man behind *In Living Color* was Keenen Ivory Wayans – a member of one of the most talented black families in comedy. Not only was he the show's creator, the man who brought the film *I'm Gonna Git you Sucka* – a blaxploitation spoof – to movie theatres also had a hand in writing and directing the television project.

Also involved in the programme were Keenen's equally creative siblings. His sister Kim and his brothers Shawn and Damon, whom years later would have a hit TV show of his own with the sitcom *My Wife and Kids,* made a significant contribution. Young comedians who had a bolder, more in-your-face type of humour were regulars on *In Living Color* developing what would become a

MAKING IT IN LA

loyal following. The cast included Jamie Foxx and (later) Chris Rock, both now popular African-American comics who, like many of their contemporaries, were able to parody and borrow from hip-hop culture. As if that wasn't enough, *In Living Color* boasted yet another achievement. It unleashed the rubber-faced talent of Jim Carrey on an unsuspecting mass audience and became a launch pad for his subsequent successful movie career.

But there was one more element that made *In Living Color* different to any other sketch show out there. Its urban flavour was completed by the inclusion of a group of funky dancers sent out to entertain the viewers in-between the comedy sketches. They were the Fly Girls and the actress and dancer Rosie Perez choreographed their energetic hip-hop moves.

These events were taking place in Los Angeles, a world away from the life of Jennifer Lopez. Back in New York the young dancer was desperate for her big break to emerge so that she could realise her dream of becoming a star. Still in her early 20s her life as a professional dancer was bringing her moderate success. She frequently appeared in the background of music videos, but she won no particular roles that would single her out, that would deliver the recognition she craved.

Friends and fellow dance students from the Phil Black Studio noted that the Jennifer who returned from the *Golden Musicals of Broadway* European tour was a different woman. Her desire, her need, to be successful was more urgent, her determination even more acute. Yet the big break she desperately chased seemed, for a time, to elude her. At first an opportunity presented itself in the hit Broadway musical *A Chorus Line*. The story, which is about a director who is casting dancers for a large stage production, must have been one close to Jennifer's heart. And the part of Diana Morales, a Latin-American dancer from the Bronx, could have been written for her. Who could play that part better than Jennifer Lopez? Wasn't that her experience dramatised on stage but embodied in a woman with a different name?

Unfortunately Jennifer's break would not come in the form of a Broadway musical. Those who knew her at the time say her failure to win the role left her a little dispirited. Despite this setback work was not in short supply. Jennifer had other projects ahead of her and she would go on to tour Japan in a show called *Synchronicity*,

MAKING IT IN LA

but it still wasn't the vehicle that she was looking for. She did not know what it was, or what form it would take. All she knew is that her opportunity had yet to arrive.

Around that time one of the original members of the Fly Girls left *In Living Color* and the show's makers were looking for a replacement. In a move that would probably be the basis for a reality TV programme today a nationwide search for a new member of the group began. Thousands of women across America rushed to audition for the job.

The credentials for a Fly Girl could easily have been adjectives used to describe Jennifer Lopez at the time. 'Fly' was the Nineties' version of the words 'cool' or 'hip'. A Fly Girl had to have attitude. She had to be slick, spunky, someone who knew she was unique, who had her own style. She was someone that men would want to 'hook up with', a chick who knew how to handle herself. Most importantly she had to have the energy to keep up with the demands of a fast-paced show. This was not ballroom dancing. The moves had to be tight and funky, the type that would not seem out of place in a hip-hop video. The new recruit had to have something that would make viewers want to keep watching, because her name and face would be familiar to thousands across the country. In fact the Fly Girls were an essential part of *In Living Color*. Unlike the background dancers of traditional sketch or variety shows each one had a 'personality' that was as recognisable to the audience back home as the faces of Jim Carrey and Damon Wayans.

Jennifer Lopez did not have to be told twice that her moment had come. In 1991 she joined 2,000 other hopefuls in New York and auditioned to become a Fly Girl. Her big break was so close she could touch it. In typical Lopez style she went out there and gave the judges everything she had. It was enough to secure her place in the final stages of the selection process, but not enough to get her the job. Jennifer was one of three finalists flown to LA to try out for the vacancy and, as the numbers were whittled down to the last two, her competitor was chosen to join the show. Frustratingly it was another near miss. Jennifer flew out to Japan to meet her other commitments.

There are countless examples throughout history where the game of 'what if' could be played. Flick through the pages of the past and they are encountered at every turn. What would have happened if Vivien Leigh failed to persistently pursue the part of Scarlett O'Hara and the role had gone to Bette Davis instead? Would the film classic *Gone with the Wind* have been the same? And if Elvis Presley had not died of a heart attack at the age of 42 would he still be swivelling his hips on *Top of the Pops* as a 21st century ageing granddaddy?

It is the same with the story of Jennifer Lopez. Where would she be today if the universe had dangled a prize in front of her, given it to someone else and left her alone with a collection of unfulfilled dreams? Who knows? All that matters is that by some twist of fate the original winner of the nationwide search for a Fly Girl competition could not take the job and it was offered to the runner-up, Jennifer, instead.

Did she still want to do it? Was she prepared to relocate to Los Angeles? And could she be on a plane as soon as possible? Yes. Yes. Yes.

If Jennifer Lopez thought that her first ride on the show business merry-go-round was going to be an easy one she was truly mistaken. Her first sacrifice was to leave New York and move to the other side of America to Los Angeles where *In Living Color* was filmed. Aged 21 she had to go where the work was and that meant leaving her family, her friends and the city of her birth,

MAKING IT IN LA

behind. The wrench was not an easy one but Jennifer, feisty as ever, was determined to savour the moment she had long anticipated.

Old clips of Jennifer Lopez as a Fly Girl on *In Living Color* reveal a woman who looks far different from the polished superstar of today. She still had a little puppy fat clinging to her face and hips. Her hair, its natural deep brown, was awash with bouncy curls when it had not been chopped into a weighty boyish cut. Even her eyebrows were less than svelte – chunky and rich chocolate in colour they came into their own when her look was completed with a swipe of red lipstick. She could look dark, mysterious, the stereotypical sultry senorita but one who had a ball of energy that oozed through every one of her pores. You could see it in her facial expressions as she stomped out the dance steps. She could look mean when she wanted to, sassy when the choreography demanded it and seduce the camera with a lingering gaze if required.

Behind the scenes, like all the other Fly Girls, Jennifer rehearsed day and night until all their routines were perfect. What looked easy to the audience at home was actually a combination of elaborate steps and choreographer Rosie Perez not only demanded that the girls got them right but that they delivered them with attitude.

By the time the final episode of *In Living Color* was aired in 1994 Jennifer Lopez was on the way to making a name for herself in the entertainment industry. The show was a stepping stone for her, a platform to get her noticed and she remained on it for only two seasons. By the time she left she was already seeking to broaden her skills, to take the leap from dancing to acting. Even from the early days of Jennifer's career, when she was on the *Golden Musicals of Broadway* tour in Europe, it was obvious that she had set herself that goal. When she called her mother in tears, complaining because she did not get a singing solo in the show it was out of frustration. She had this vision of herself that went beyond dancing.

Jennifer's next endeavour would take her a step closer to that vision. A fellow Fly Girl and New Yorker was a friend of Janet Jackson and had become part of the singer's team of dancers. She suggested that Jennifer join the group and the former Bronx native was soon performing with an artist she had long admired from afar. For the 1993 video *That's the Way Love Goes* she appears as one of Janet's friends who encourage her to sing her

MAKING IT IN LA

latest single while they lounge around, dance and nod their approval. She must have been doing a good job because by the time Janet Jackson was ready to begin her world tour she wanted to take Jennifer with her. But by then another opportunity had presented itself to the dancer – one that would take her career to the next level.

Another fellow Fly Girl was married to a producer who was writing and producing a pilot for television called *South Central*. The show was based on the trials of a single mother, her two teenage children and a five-year-old foster child. The family were based in South Central, Los Angeles and it was supposed to be a realistic look at what life was like for them, but with an undercurrent of humour. The part that Jennifer was invited to read for was that of Lucy, the single mother's work colleague at the local grocery store. She was required to bring elements of her own personality to the role of a strong, spirited Latina. The producer, realising that Jennifer was who he was looking for, offered her the part.

The rapidity with which Jennifer's career was progressing was astounding. It wasn't so long ago that she was living in New York actively searching for her big break as a dancer, wondering when someone was going to notice her. Now, five years after she set her heart on making it in the entertainment industry, she was in a choice position. Should she jump on a plane and go to Europe as a dancer on Janet Jackson's world tour or should she take the role of Lucy in *South Central*? She agonised over the decision but in the end opted for the television show.

She made the right choice. While the television network CBS did not want *South Central* – which later had a short run on Fox – they did want Jennifer. The station's former head, Jeff Sagansky, was so impressed with her performance that he offered her a deal. Fox gave her a year's contract while they tried to find another programme to showcase her talent. That show was the drama *Second Chances*, which featured Jennifer as Melinda Lopez, a young woman trying to live her life and find happiness despite her overprotective father. That programme lasted slightly longer than *South Central*, but was also short-lived and eventually became *Hotel Malibu*. Although Jennifer's character now became the focal point of the show it failed to attract a large following. The young actress was not perturbed. By the time *Hotel Malibu* came to an end she had set her sights

MAKING IT IN LA

on another goal – she was transferring her talents from television to the big screen.

As first films go Jennifer Lopez's real debut[1] on the big screen was an impressive one. Directed by Gregory Nava *My Family, Mi Familia* traced the fortunes of three generations of a Mexican-American family based in California. It was an ambitious piece that covered several periods in history from the Twenties right through to the Nineties. A critical success, it boasted a stellar cast with Jimmy Smits and Edward James Olmos (most famous for his performance in the 1988 film *Stand and Deliver*) co-starring. Most actresses would give their left arm to make a screen debut in such esteemed company.

Jennifer's on-screen performance as Maria Sanchez in her first film has been hailed as one of her best. It was also one of her least glamourous and most emotionally demanding roles. Her soon to be famous figure was not on display in an array of barely-there costumes. Her face was stripped of make-up. No diamonds adorned her fingers. Instead she played the wife of a Hispanic immigrant who, in the Twenties, is shipped back to central Mexico. The challenge she faces is to return with her child to California. The role called

MAKING IT IN LA

for her to display an emotional range that few of her previous on-screen characters tapped into.

Released in 1995 *My Family, Mi Familia* was Jennifer's calling card. In four short years she had gone from being a Fly Girl, to one of Janet Jackson's dancers, to a television actress and now a Hollywood starlet. At 25 she must have been overjoyed at her level of success. She would soon have a greater cause for celebration. As her movie career unfolded, not only would she work with some of the most respected actors and directors in the business she would carve out a position for herself and earn her place in history all at the same time.

1. Jennifer's first film appearance was in the 1986 movie *My Little Girl* in which she had a small part.

7

Selena

JENNIFER LOPEZ

SELENA

Ask any aspiring actress in Hollywood to put together a wish list of the people she would like to work with during the course of her career and 90 per cent of the entries would be predictable. Most of them would be Oscar winners like Jack Nicholson, Michael Caine and Sean Penn. Funny-man Robin Williams might be on there, while the directors Oliver Stone and Francis Ford Coppola would definitely make an appearance. A little further down, maybe, would be the names Woody Harrelson and Wesley Snipes, especially if the list had been compiled in the early Nineties soon after the pair appeared in the comedy *White Men Can't Jump*.

For a young actress finding her feet in Hollywood, sharing the screen with the catalogue of stars above would seem, quite rightly, a long way off. The list, once written, would be tucked away in a little box and every three or four years, when one of the goals had been achieved it would be taken out for the names to be crossed off. Not so for Jennifer Lopez. After the release of her first film in 1995 she was able to put a tick by each of those names within three years.

After *My Family, Mi Familia* her next film was *Money Train*, a buddy cops movie that starred Woody Harrelson and Wesley Snipes. By doing this project she followed in the footsteps of her Fly Girls choreographer Rosie Perez, who had appeared with the duo in their 1992 venture *White Men Can't Jump*. Unfortunately *Money Train* was not a box office hit, but Jennifer's portrayal of undercover police officer Grace Santiago was well received.

Her next project would see her working with the man behind *The Godfather* trilogy, Francis Ford Coppola, in his 1996 comedy *Jack*. *Jack* (played by Robin Williams) was the story of a 10-year-old boy with a growth disorder that made him age four times faster than normal. He meets Jennifer's character (his teacher) when he goes to state school for the first time as a child who looks like a 40-year-old man.

Jennifer's ability to hold her own on-screen (and behind the camera) speaks volumes about her ability not to be overwhelmed by the reputation of her colleagues but to focus on the task at hand grasping the opportunity to learn, grow and develop her craft further. Armed with her own brand of self-belief she did not cave in under pressure. Instead she demystified the whole process declaring to the *Los Angeles Daily News* that Coppola was like a "teddy bear" who created a "nurturing atmosphere" on set.

Her experience working with Francis Ford Coppola and Robin Williams served her well because in her next film she worked alongside two more Hollywood greats – Jack Nicholson and Michael Caine in *Blood and Wine*. From there she went on to shoot *Anaconda*, an action thriller about a group of documentary filmmakers terrorised by a giant snake in the Amazon rainforest. Her co-stars this time were Jon Voight, rapper-turned-actor Ice Cube, Eric Stoltz and Owen Wilson. It was her first box office smash.

SELENA

In a few short years Jennifer Lopez had built up an impressive body of work as a young actress. She moved deftly between different movie genres. She could do drama, comedy, film noir and big-action money-spinners. Whatever the role required she could bring it to the table. It was a combination designed to make studio bosses take notice. It was to her credit that while they were noticing her talent her race became less important. While she was, and is, immensely proud to be a Latina, in Hollywood true power as an ethnic minority actor comes when producers and directors see beyond colour. The possibilities become endless when, despite her race, an actress is hired to play the 'female lead' instead of being left on the shelf, only to be pulled out when an 'ethnic part' surfaces. Right from the start of her film career Jennifer bounced between roles that required a Latin actress, like Maria Sanchez in *My Family, Mi Familia,* to others where race was incidental, as it was in *Money Train.* Her position as an actress that major Hollywood players wanted to work with was solidified when film director Oliver Stone came to her, proposal in hand. He wanted her to appear in his next project, *U Turn.* Sharon Stone was said to be interested in the part that Jennifer eventually won – that of Grace McKenna, a woman who is married to one of the most powerful men in a small Arizona town. Her husband Jake (played by Nick Nolte) wants her killed and offers Bobby Cooper (Sean Penn) money to do the job, before Jennifer's character suggests the hit man makes her a widow instead.

If the race of the female lead was of little importance in *U Turn* it was of major significance to the next project Jennifer would undertake – the dramatisation of the life of Selena.

On the morning of 31 March 1995 a 23-year-old woman was shot in her back at a Days Inn hotel in Corpus Christi, Texas. The assailant was a registered nurse in her early 30s called Yolanda Saldivar. The victim was her former friend and employer Selena Quintanilla Perez. By the time the young woman was rushed to hospital she was pronounced dead on arrival. The death prompted an outpouring of grief in her local town and in the Latin-American community around the world. The scene of Selena's murder quickly became a shrine, prayer vigils were held and people came to the streets in a spontaneous outpouring of collective grief.

JENNIFER LOPEZ

SELENA

The name of the woman who died was unfamiliar to the majority of Anglo-Americans, but to the Hispanic community she was a superstar and their display of public emotion was akin to the scenes that followed the murder of John Lennon. At times described as the Mexican Madonna or hailed as the next Gloria Estefan, Selena was like the Beyoncé Knowles of Tejano music. In that male dominated field she had sailed to the top, breaking down barriers at every turn. The little girl from Corpus Christi, who had sung throughout her childhood, had blossomed into a Grammy award winning, platinum album selling artist who in the month before her death played before 60,000 fans in her home state of Texas. And she was about to become an even bigger star as success in the 'mainstream' entertainment world beckoned. Selena had just made her movie debut in *Don Juan De Marco* in a small part alongside Marlon Brando and Johnny Depp and she was halfway through recording her English language crossover album. Then, suddenly, she was gone.

Had her life not been wrenched away from her Selena would have been leading the Latin wave that was soon to consume the American pop charts. What Beyoncé and Jennifer Lopez have

SELENA

since done for voluptuous women of colour by unashamedly celebrating their curves, Selena would have achieved that little bit earlier. On stage she performed in tight trousers and bustiers, never hiding her self away but never revealing too much either. To men she was a sex symbol. To young girls she was a role model, a performer and business woman who also had a range of clothing boutiques to her name.

All this potential was cut short by the actions of Yolanda Saldivar. The Quintanilla family had accused Saldivar, the former president of Selena's fan club, of embezzling funds from the organisation. When Selena was shot she was going to meet Yolanda to view documents the registered nurse assured her would prove her innocence.

The violent way Selena died was a heady mix of drama and tragedy – a ready made screenplay crying out to be filmed. The result was a Warner Bros production that the Quintanilla family were closely involved in. All that was left was to find the right person to play the title role.

Hollywood folklore has it that every Latino actress with a drop of ambition in their blood wanted to play Selena. It was a challenge for any casting director to undertake. Not only had the

SELENA

film's heroine recently died (the movie was released in 1997 two year's after the singer's killing) her image was still fresh in people's minds. Add to that the fact that Selena was so adored by her fans that any woman assuming the role would undoubtedly face some form of criticism from a grief-stricken community still reeling from shock and the enormity of the task becomes apparent. Who could embody Selena? With her cascading dark hair and red pout she already had movie star good looks. But what about her aura, her down-to-earth charm, her ability to fill up a stage with her carefree dance moves? Who could become all those things?

Realising their dilemma the filmmakers, determined to cast the right person, widened their search beyond the boundaries of LA. They held open auditions in Texas, California, Illnois and Florida to find the right two actors to play Selena as a child and as an adult. Thousands of young women descended on the casting calls to try their luck.

Jennifer Lopez was one of the many actresses in Hollywood who read for the part but she had something that made her stand out Abraham Quintanilla, Selena's father, who was heavily

SELENA

involved in bringing his daughter's story to the big screen, was struck by the similarities between the two women. The filmmakers also felt that she embodied the slain singer's spirit, that their lives in some ways mirrored each other. Both women were around the same age. (Selena, just shy of her 24th birthday when she died, was nine months younger than Jennifer.) They both possessed the drive and ambition necessary to succeed. They were passionate about their work yet love of family was central to their being. Each had notched up several successes in their careers but was set for bigger things. Throw in Jennifer's skill as a dancer and it is obvious why she won the coveted part.

But, in doing so, she had achieved much more than the title role in a major production. Jennifer was paid $1million for her performance making her the highest paid Hispanic actress in the world. Still in her mid-20s the girl from Castle Hill, the Bronx had made history.

The expected backlash was swift in coming. The main criticism levelled at the casting choice was Jennifer's background. How could the producers choose a Latin-American of Puerto Rican descent to portray a Mexican-American

SELENA

woman? Jennifer set about answering her critics the best way she knew how; by working hard and doing as much research as possible. She worked with the film's choreographer to unlearn her trained dance instincts and reproduce Selena's improvisational style. She slept, ate, lived and breathed Selena. At every opportunity she played her CDs. The Quintanilla family were adamant that Selena's voice would be heard so Jennifer would not sing on film but she would have to master the art of effective lip-synching.

Perhaps the most important preparation that Jennifer undertook for the role was to spend time with the Quintanilla family in a bid to capture the essence of their loved one. Selena was by no means a one-woman band. Her family – her brother, sister, father and mother – were heavily involved in the production of her records and live performances. Her siblings played with her on stage. Her brother co-produced and co-wrote many of her hit records. Her father, Abraham, encouraged his children to get into the music business in the first place and went on to manage them when they became Selena y Los Dinos. There was a lifetime of home videos, stories and photos for Jennifer to view within the Quintanilla household. Every

SELENA

resource was made available to her.

In front of the camera Jennifer put all that knowledge to good use. Abraham Quintanilla has gone on record to say that at certain stages in the production of *Selena* he was stunned by the ability of the actress to bring his daughter to life. Jennifer had captured everything, all the little nuances the singer had. It was the way she giggled, the way she moved her head, the way she smiled or held her own on stage, the very look in her eye. It was convincing enough to reduce Selena's mother to tears.

Jennifer's hard work paid large dividends. The film *Selena* was another box office smash that earned her critical acclaim. In 1998 she was nominated for a Golden Globe for best actress and an MTV Movie Award for best breakthrough performance. She won neither but the recognition was welcomed. In the same year she won a Lone Star Film and Television Award and an ALMA (Association for Latin-American Music and Art), both for best actress in *Selena*.

Jennifer Lopez, the movie star, had landed. She had surpassed many of the goals that she had set for herself, leaving the expectations that others had for her far behind. She had pushed herself to

SELENA

develop as an artist and now the former Fly Girl had proven to Hollywood that she could carry a film. Her next two projects demonstrated how far she had come. In 1998 she played the love interest of heart-throb George Clooney in Steven Soderbergh's dark romantic comedy *Out of Sight*. The on-screen chemistry between the two was electric and Jennifer's portrayal of the conflicting sides of US Marshal Karen Sisco, earned her a reputation as a sex symbol in her own right. Audiences loved the contrasting elements she gave the character – the tough and the smooth, the confident vulnerability of a woman reluctant to let her guard down.

She went from lending her body to the film *Out of Sight* to lending her voice to the animated film *Antz*. Again she was in esteemed company. Her co-stars included Woody Allen, Dan Ackroyd, Anne Bancroft, Danny Glover and Gene Hackman.

With these many accomplishments under her belt no one would blame Jennifer Lopez for wanting to step back, take a break and enjoy what she had achieved. Her star had risen at a breakneck speed, surely there was nothing else professionally that she needed to reach for beyond an Academy Award? There was. And it was while

J-Lo appearing at the MTV awards, Stockholm, Sweden (2000).

Jennifer Lopez has proved herself as an accomplished singer, dancer, actor, songwriter and entrepreneur, with a string of hit singles, films and her own perfume and clothing line.

J-Lo and Ralph Fiennes from a scene from the popular 2003 film 'Maid in Manhattan'.

The relationship between Jennifer Lopez and Ben Affleck was not to last and the couple parted company in early 2004.

SELENA

she was on the set of *Selena* that an old desire she had long held within her resurfaced. Jennifer did not just want to be a dancer/actress. She was reaching for that old style Hollywood glamour and wanted to become an all round entertainer – a dancer/actress/singer. There was one more challenge to meet, one remaining industry to conquer – the music business.

But before she could achieve that ultimate goal she would be married, divorced and then connected to one of the biggest names in hip-hop.

8

Ojani and Puff

JENNIFER LOPEZ

OJANI AND PUFF

The month was January. The year was 1998. The event was the Golden Globe Awards in Los Angeles, one of the most important dates in Tinseltown's annual calendar. Each year, on that night, the stars come out in all their regalia in a test run for the Oscars. For the ladies their outfits are exquisite, but not as grand as the ones they are going to wear at the Academy Awards. Everyone in Hollywood – producers, directors, screenwriters, studio bosses, actors and actresses alike – wait, bottoms perched on the edge of their seats, to see which movies are going to walk away with the major prizes. For it is often said that the Golden

OJANI AND PUFF

Globes are the precursors to the Oscars. And whoever wins the three biggies – best actor, best actress, best picture – in this round are a step closer to joining one of the most exclusive clubs in town, the Academy of Motion Picture, Arts and Sciences.

That night in particular Hollywood was celebrating a bumper crop of quality movies. Over the previous 12 months cinemagoers were treated to James Cameron's epic, *Titanic,* a disaster-cum-romantic tale starring Leonardo DiCaprio and Kate Winslet. Jack Nicholson showed that he was still in the game with his portrayal of an obsessive-compulsive writer in *As Good as it Gets*. Burt Reynolds boosted his career as well with *Boogie Nights,* a look at the porn industry. It was also the year that America's sweetheart, Julia Roberts, starred in the comedy *My Best Friend's Wedding* and Hollywood first fell in love with Russell Crowe in *LA Confidential.* Crowe was not the only newcomer who created a buzz that night. Two little-known actors would walk away with the Golden Globe for best screenplay for their critically acclaimed offering, *Good Will Hunting*. The winners of that award were Matt Damon and Ben Affleck.

JENNIFER LOPEZ

OJANI AND PUFF

The romance between Ben and Jen (as they would become known in the tabloids) was a lifetime away, however. On that night few of the viewers watching the ceremony around the globe knew who Jennifer Lopez was. She had been nominated alongside Helen Hunt, Pam Grier and Julia Roberts in the Actress in a Leading Role in a Musical or Comedy category for her performance in *Selena*. But who was she? Despite the seven films that Jennifer had appeared in, beyond the confines of Hollywood, cinemagoers largely recognised her face, not her name. That would all change after the 1998 Golden Globes. That night was the night of Jennifer Lopez and although Helen Hunt walked away with the award her fellow nominee grabbed the media's attention with her stunning Valentino gown.

Pictures of Jennifer taken that night demonstrate how easily she had slipped into the role of movie star. She did Hollywood glamour with poise. Like a latter-day Marilyn Monroe she must have known that when she poured her body into that skintight number she was going to cause a sensation. The dress in question was a sleeveless off the shoulder gown that had a triangular-shaped slash in the middle exposing her midriff. It did its job for both actress and designer – it didn't fade into the background in a sea of black, instead its yellow top and purple and lavender bottom caught the rays of multiple flashbulbs. Most importantly the dress hung on every curve of Jennifer's body. It caressed her boobs, hugged her tummy, and traced the shape of her bottom before it fell, a whisper away from her thighs. The tomboyish 'Fly Girl' had metamorphosed into a beautiful and confident actress who was in complete control of her image. Gone was the puppy fat. In its place was a toned, yet curvaceous body that could have stepped out of Fifties' Hollywood. Jennifer stood out from many of her contemporaries, not only because she did not fit into the California beach blonde dieted-to-within-an-inch-of-your-life mould, but also because she was unwilling to force herself into that category. She did not hide away her generous bottom, hips and thighs – traits that the Latino and African-American communities hold as desirable. She celebrated them. Her dress, the poses she adopted, the look in her eyes spoke of a woman happy with herself, her curves and her place in the world.

Jennifer had an additional reason to feel happy that night. She was in love. The man holding her hand as she walked down the red

OJANI AND PUFF

carpet was Ojani Noa – her husband.

The great irony about Jennifer Lopez is, as boyfriends go, she has lived a relatively chaste life. J-Lo, the great sex symbol, who in the future would be mocked in the press for the swiftness with which she parts from husbands and lovers, in reality has had only a handful of committed relationships.

One of her longest romantic partnerships was with her first true love, David Cruz. He was a local boy who Jennifer got together with at the age of 15 when she was still at high school back in the Bronx. The couple was devoted to each other and when her career dictated that she move to Los Angeles he quickly followed her. Unfortunately, as Jennifer's career developed, their relationship cracked under the strain and, after a decade together, they split up. David returned to New York to start a dry cleaning business while Jennifer conceded that the demands of the industry contributed to their break-up. She told *Latina* magazine it was difficult for her ex to see her romantically involved with other men on screen.

The whirlwind nature of Jennifer's next relationship could have been plucked from one of her movies in which a fairytale love scene was the

OJANI AND PUFF

centrepiece. She met her next man in Miami halfway through the filming of *Blood and Wine*. She was a Hollywood starlet who, by day, was playing Jack Nicholson's lover. He was a Cuban immigrant who worked as a waiter in Gloria Estefan's restaurant, the scene of their meeting. His name was Ojani and he had no idea who she was. Jennifer, devoid of any snobbery that might suggest a waiter was beneath her, was mesmerised by his good looks and charm.

By the time *Selena* was being filmed Jennifer and Ojani were dating. By the time the female lead had said her goodbyes to cast and crew, they were engaged. At the wrap party for *Selena*, as music played in the background, Ojani grabbed a microphone and made his way to the dance floor. Once there, he got down on his knees and proposed to her. Jennifer said yes. It seemed the natural thing to do. Life seemed perfect. She was the highest paid Latino actress in Hollywood history. She had just wrapped the most important film of her career and now the man she was in love with asked her to marry him. On 22 February 1997 Jennifer Lopez walked down the aisle for the first time. Sadly the marriage would not see the end of 1998.

JENNIFER LOPEZ

OJANI AND PUFF

Again it seems that Jennifer's romantic attachments could not compete with the demands of her career. Twice she had tried to be involved with men not in the entertainment industry. Twice it had ended in failure. The natural conclusion would be to become involved with a man more like herself – someone who was submerged in the business, who too was a perfectionist and a workaholic; someone like Sean 'Puffy' Combs.

The rumours about Jennifer Lopez and Puff Daddy started to fly in 1997 when she was still married to Ojani Noa. No one could blame the media and the public for jumping to conclusions when they saw the video for Puff's single *Been Around the World,* taken from his platinum selling debut album *No Way Out*. The video featured Jennifer as a beautiful princess – she even had her own throne. The climax of their first professional collaboration was their on-screen dance number. To say it was steamy is an understatement. Puff, dressed all in black with his shirt slashed to his waist, held his own with Jennifer as they did the salsa around a candlelit set. As Jennifer recalls they did not have much rehearsal time, but they didn't need it. The chemistry was such that the number went off without a hitch. Gossipmongers,

OJANI AND PUFF

salivating at the sight, predicted a relationship that in reality would only blossom once Jennifer had divorced Ojani.

Although celebrity-watchers would not initially pair rap mogul up with Hollywood's highest paid Latin actress in hindsight theirs was a natural match. Their similarities outweighed their differences. Though he was black and she was Hispanic, African-Americans and Latin-Americans share similar backgrounds. The two communities often live in the same inner city pockets of America and both races have faced the twin evils of marginalisation and prejudice. Jennifer and Puff also had the same home city in common – New York. She was from the Bronx, he was born in Harlem. And although he was the son of a murdered drug dealer their familial morals were not dissimilar. Puff's mother worked night and day to send her son to a fee-paying school and his grandmother ingrained in him a love of God. They were connected on other levels. At the time of their first professional union Jennifer had moved from the world of dance to the field of acting and was on the cusp of moving into the music business. Puffy, the CEO of Bad Boy Records, had taken a walk from behind the mixing desks to behind the

OJANI AND PUFF

mike, elevating himself from hip-hop producer to rap artist with impressive results. They had both come a long way from their early days as background dancers in music videos.

It was their mutual appreciation of each other's work that brought them together. Jennifer told VH1 that when Puff approached her to appear in his music video she had had no desire to return to that format (presumably until she could showcase her own vocal talent). But the actress had long been one of his fans so she seized the opportunity. On his part, Puff said it was the movie *Selena* that set the light bulb off in his head to cast Jennifer in *Been Around the World*. It was her ability to move that caught his attention and, remembering that she used to be a dancer, he approached her.

Two years would go by before producer and actress confessed to a romantic relationship. It would not be until Jennifer had amicably divorced from Ojani and Puff had separated from Kim Porter – the mother of his second son, Christian – that they stepped out together publicly. Between that date and the *Been Around the World* video Jennifer would give birth to *On the 6*.

Ava Gardner had Frank Sinatra, Lauren

JENNIFER LOPEZ

OJANI AND PUFF

Bacall had Humphrey Bogart and Marilyn Monroe – well, take your pick. The blonde bombshell had baseball player Joe DiMaggio, the playwright Arthur Miller and the Kennedy brothers, attorney general and president of the United States, Bobby and John F. The point is the legendary Hollywood glamour queens who graced the town in its golden age all had their match, their male equivalent, someone who they would forever be associated with or attached to. As she took her first steps into the limelight, Jennifer Lopez would be no different. Like Marilyn Monroe her first husband was an 'average Joe', an 'ordinary' man with an 'ordinary' job. When Jennifer's name first became linked with that of Puff Daddy she had found her Bogart.

9

On the six

ON THE SIX

Dressed in a purple catsuit Jennifer Lopez entered the Houston Astrodome and was met by the thunderous roar of a 60,000-strong crowd. She hopped onto a horse-drawn carriage and did a lap of honour smiling and waving at her audience along the way. The carriage deposited her at a circular stage where a live band stood, all warmed up ready to accompany her. As the band started playing she broke into a version of Gloria Gayner's disco classic *I Will Survive*. The crowd cheered their appreciation. They waved banners and called out the name of the woman they had come to see. But that name was not Jennifer

ON THE SIX

Lopez, or even J-Lo, it was Selena. And this was not a real concert it was a scene from the movie of the Tejano singer's life – a recreation of the night of 26 February 1995, the last opportunity fans would get to see her perform live. In fact the extras on the set were all Selena fans. They had not come for Jennifer Lopez. They had come to support their idol – to keep the memory of one they loved so dearly alive.

The crowd may not have been chanting her name or responding to her talents as a singer, but for Jennifer the effect was the same. The rush of emotion she felt on set that day was incomparable to any other she had experienced before. Neither acting nor dancing had given her the opportunity to interact with an audience who responded immediately to what she did on stage. Never before had she experienced that level of adoration, that cocktail of excitement and hysteria that only music fans can bring to a live gig. Legend has it that after she filmed the Houston Astrodome scene Jennifer turned to her colleagues on set that day and asserted that she too wanted to become a singer. She was inspired. Though she herself did not say it, it seemed that history had in some way anointed her and she would be the one to take up

ON THE SIX

the baton dropped by Selena on the day she died. Jennifer could never replace her, but she could fulfil the promise that others saw in the slain star by becoming the biggest mainstream Latin-American female vocalist since Gloria Estefan. Other Hispanic women had taken to the stage since Gloria first broke through in the Eighties – Mariah Carey is one example – but Jennifer, like Selena, would bring the richness of her culture to the pop charts.

In reality Jennifer had had her sights set on a recording career long before the filming of *Selena* came to pass. Around the time that she was dancing with Janet Jackson she approached Giant Records in search of a record deal. Even then, in the early Nineties, she had a clear vision of the type of artist she wanted to be. Like Britney Spears and Justin Timberlake a few years later she wanted to build upon the entertainment standard set by the pop stars of the Eighties. Like Madonna, Janet Jackson and her brother Michael, Jennifer wanted to bring to videos and to the stage the artistry of an all-round performer. She would combine all the elements that made her who she was – the singing and the dancing, the hip-hop and R&B mixed in with the salsa and merengue.

ON THE SIX

Giant Records did not rush to offer Jennifer a deal, but her stock was greater after the release of *Selena* when Tommy Mottola, the CEO of Sony Music Entertainment, offered her a recording contract, which she accepted. With Tommy overseeing her music career Jennifer was virtually guaranteed success on the pop charts. The list of household names Mottola had brought to the public's attention when he was at the helm of Sony was an impressive one. Destiny's Child, Michael Bolton, Celine Dion and Ricky Martin were all signed during the Mottola era. But one of the most successful careers that Tommy ever guided was that of his ex-wife Mariah Carey. The oft-repeated story goes that an 18-year-old Mariah, then a back-up singer for R&B artist Brenda K Starr, handed Tommy her demo tape at a music industry party. He took the tape, played it in his car on the way home and was so impressed with her voice that he got his driver to turn the car around so he could return to the party and track down the mystery girl. A record deal swiftly followed and Mariah became one of the most successful female recording artists of her generation. In America, every year of the Nineties was christened with a Mariah Carey number one. Her debut album alone

ON THE SIX

spawned four chart toppers and two Grammy awards. If Jennifer could replicate one tenth of Carey's success she would make a huge impact on the music world. The astounding achievements of the former Mrs Tommy Mottola would be a big enough incentive for any artist to seek shelter under the wing of Sony's chief executive. Any album conceived in this professional union was headed for success.

As always with Jennifer rumours surrounded her involvement with Tommy. They were both newly single and speculation grew that, like Mariah, her relationship with Mottola would develop outside the studio. As salacious as that gossip was a romantic union between the two was never on the cards. Their partnership was strictly business. They shared a similar vision – Jennifer wanted to harness her talents to produce the best debut album she possibly could and Tommy was willing to invest in her to make that happen. The producers and songwriters brought on board to make that vision a reality demonstrated his commitment to the project. Corey Rooney, Emilio Estefan (the husband and creative partner of Gloria), Rodney Jerkins and, of course, Sean 'Puffy' Combs all loaned their talents to the album.

ON THE SIX

Between them this collection of music makers had worked with the crème de la crème of the industry – from power-balladeers Celine Dion and Whitney Houston to the raw vocals of Mary J Blige through to the poster girls for the next generation, former teenyboppers Brandy and Monica.

Other artists came on board to support Jennifer's vision. Gloria Estefan gave her a song that she had written for her own album, *Let's Get Loud* – a bold Latin pop number with African-Caribbean beats. On *Feelin' so Good*, an R&B inspired song recalling her life in the Bronx, the lyrical abilities of Hispanic rappers Big Pun and Fat Joe were harnessed. For the romantic ballad *No Me Ames* Jennifer was partnered with Latin superstar Marc Anthony (another man who, again, she would later be connected with).

No matter how much money a record company throws at a project or how many accomplished songwriters, producers and musicians come on board, if the person carrying the album has no vocal talent their efforts will only produce a short burst of success with no hope of long-term achievement. It is something that real music enthusiasts can easily detect. Far greater actors than Jennifer Lopez have tried to add the title of singer to their CVs and failed with embarrassing results. The number of soap, film and sitcom stars who have attempted that leap only to fall on their face is enough to fill the pages of an encyclopedia. Jennifer was determined not to be one of them. While she was confident in her ability as a singer and bolstered by the backing of Tommy Mottola et al she knew that, at best, she would amount to a one hit wonder if she was not prepared to work hard. Her film career was put on hold while she spent hours and the best part of a year in the recording studio. If she was ever tempted to take the pressure off herself, to relax, she remembered that a hungry media waited outside, eager to shoot her down if the efforts of this latest actor-turned-pop-star-wannabe were anything but the best.

An engineer working on the album told VH1 that Jennifer would be at the studio first thing in the morning and last thing at night, breaking only to go to the gym to work out. Also, confident that she was working with people more experienced than her, she was not too proud to take direction. When she was told that some singers prefer to work in a studio free from electric lights, lit only by candles to create a more creative atmosphere, she acquiesced. Jennifer was also receptive to the

ON THE SIX

guidance of her producers who, like directors on a film set, encouraged her to get into the right mood to communicate the emotions of the songs to her audience. As one producer, Lawrence Dermer, put it she was willing to adopt any number of vocal experiments to create the required effect, anything to ensure that her album exceeded expectations.

Jennifer's devotion to the project, her attention to detail, extended to how the collection of songs was to be packaged. When Tony Duran, the album's photographer came on board, she told him that she was willing to follow every one of his directions. She was the novice. He was the expert. In this instance his knowledge and experience were superior to hers. Tony did not face a diva with demanding requests telling him how her face should be lit or from which angle it would be best shot. On the contrary, he met a woman confident enough to take direction from others when the situation demanded it. Whatever it took to make her voice sound good on the album or to make the pictures that adorned the cover stunning she was prepared to do.

It is at this point that the J-Lo brand began to emerge. Jennifer was going to put her name to this album, her image was going to be on the cover

ON THE SIX

and, as a result, it had to be a quality project that was an expression of her as a person and symbolic of all that she held dear. The greatest indication that this was a personal offering of herself to the public was in the title she gave to the album – *On the 6*. The six was the train that Jennifer took from the Bronx into Manhattan. Not only was it her way out of an otherwise ordinary life, it connected her to her neighbourhood, her community, the place where it all began. The six was the train that she would travel on to go to college and to and from dance auditions. As she would later do with her song *Jenny from the Block*, Jennifer Lopez was paying tribute to her roots.

The first single to be released from *On the 6* was a song co-written by Rodney Jerkins, the man behind Brandy and Monica's record-breaking 1998 US hit, *The Boy is Mine*. *If You Had My Love* was also the first track on the album; and consequently it was the first opportunity the public had to listen to Jennifer's real voice. Could the woman who lip-synched her way through *Selena* really sing? The answer was 'yes'. Her voice was not as strong as Selena's. It also lacked the range of a Mariah Carey or the gospel influence of powerhouses like Mary J Blige or

ON THE SIX

Whitney Houston, but like Madonna and Janet Jackson, Jennifer Lopez could carry a tune. Her voice, though soft and light was blessed with the twin necessities of character and emotion; it was expressive. On the first single it sailed above a string arrangement punctuated by an R&B beat. Each time she got to the chorus, asking her potential lover if he would be true to her if they got together, her concerns were reinforced by the harmony vocals of two session singers.

The arrangement was a success and when it was released in May 1999 *If You Had My Love* topped the charts in America, knocking Ricky Martin's *Livin' La Vida Loca* off the top spot in the process. It was the middle of Latin fever and Jennifer Lopez adopted the position as its chart-topping queen for five weeks. In Britain, where the single entered the charts at number four, it was voted number 10 in the record of the year competition.

Jennifer was thrilled at the success of her first single, but she was also pleased with the response to the video. It showed her performing to some of her fans who looked on from the comfort of their homes, connected to her through the Internet. Puff Daddy, Jennifer would later recall, came up with

ON THE SIX

the idea to tap into the technological wave sweeping the nation. That year the video was nominated for four MTV Video Music Awards including Best Female Video, Best Dance Video, Best Pop Video and Best New Artist.

As debut albums go the 16-track *On the 6* was quite an achievement. Two more singles were released – the dance number *Waiting for Tonight* and *Feelin' So Good,* which was co-written by Jennifer. She helped to pen three other tracks on the album – *It's Not That Serious, Should've Never* and *Too Late* – and tackled a modern-day classic, *Do You Know Where You're Going To,* the theme from the film *Mahogany*, originally sung by Diana Ross. Jennifer Lopez had made her mark as a singer, delivering her version of Latin soul to the music listening audience while swimming effortlessly between pop, R&B and dance, Spanish and English.

Having shown the world that she could sing on 10 July 1999 she showed one billion television viewers that she could give a spectacular live performance. During the opening ceremony of the Women's World Cup (Football) Finals Jennifer did a set that included *Let's Get Loud* and her number one single in front of a crowd that included Bill

ON THE SIX

Clinton, the then president of the United States.

In the 11 years since Jennifer Lopez had left her childhood home in Castle Hill, the Bronx, she had achieved all she wanted to and more. But with great success, comes great responsibility. And great responsibility brings scrutiny from a multitude of directions – from the press, various social groups and an army of adoring fans all who feel they have a claim on the artist in question. Jennifer could notch up as many box office hits and pop chart successes as she wanted to, but that did not hush the rumours circulating around her. The humble, unassuming, hardworking person that she believed herself to be was not reflected in the press, especially in Europe. At times they called her a pompous diva but the easiest charge to level at her was that she was a fickle mistress, someone who changed her lovers as regularly as most people change their underwear. In the four years between 2000 and 2004 Jennifer would inadvertently fuel media attention by having two broken engagements and another short-lived marriage. There seemed to be an inverse relationship between the successes in her professional life and the failures of her personal partnerships – the higher she would soar in the one, the deeper she would fall in the other.

10

Cris Judd

JENNIFER LOPEZ

CRIS JUDD

Jennifer Lopez and her boyfriend Puff Daddy had been stimulating media interest long before the events of 27 December 1999. Before a single shot was fired at Club New York speculation had surrounded the true nature of their friendship. In the months between her divorce from Ojani Noa and her public display of affection for Puff, Jennifer did her best to bat away any interest in her private life. Nevertheless among the list of people credited for their contribution to her first album was a message to an anonymous person known only as "my favourite". Lopez cooed about their love for each other, saying they were

CRIS JUDD

meant to be. When MTV asked her to elaborate on the identity of that special someone (could it be Puff?) Jennifer was coy, acknowledging only that she wanted to keep this relationship out of the public eye.

When the pair eventually did step out together as a couple, it was at Puff's annual Labour Day party thrown at his home in the East Hamptons. That September, both dressed in white, they were seen waving at guests from the perch of his balcony. Friends of Puff declared that he had met his match. In the VH1 *Behind the Music* documentary of his life he acknowledged that Jennifer was the female version of himself. Although he had had two important relationships that produced his sons, Justin and Christian, never before in his life had he slowed down long enough to truly appreciate a steady union. He had been too busy building his empire. Now, in Jennifer, he found someone whose drive, ambition and motivation matched his own. And the time was right for him to embark upon another serious relationship, two years after his best friend, the rapper Biggie Smalls (aka the Notorious BIG), had been gunned down.

While there was much to suggest that

CRIS JUDD

Jennifer and Puff should be together there were differing aspects of their personalities that indicated they would be better off apart. The incident at Club New York in December 1999 was symbolic of the gulf between them. Jennifer is a self-confessed homebody who does not drink or smoke. After a long day on a film set, or in the studio knocking out hits, she much prefers to relax at home in the company of family and friends rather than set the dance floor alight. Puff, on the other hand, loves to party. He works hard and plays hard and he enjoys nothing more than seeing people have a good time at his expense and at his instigation. The idea of going to Club New York that night probably appealed more to him than to his girlfriend.

Then there was the violence. That same year, before Jennifer and he were arrested in the wake of the December shooting Puff had already had his run-in with the law. In April he had been accused of attacking the record promoter Steve Stoute over his (Puff's) appearance in a video for a single released by Nas, a fellow rapper. In the scenes shot for *Hate Me Now* Puff appeared on a cross in a mock crucifixion. He said he wanted those scenes to be cut before the video was aired

CRIS JUDD

on MTV and when they were not the alleged assault took place. Puffy pleaded guilty to the charges and acknowledged his lapse in judgement before being instructed by the judge to undergo a course of anger management therapy.

Amazingly, despite these troubles, and the December 1999 shootings, Jennifer stubbornly stuck by her man. For over a year, even with the impending trial hanging over them, the union between the two artists survived. He visited her on location as she filmed *The Wedding Planner* with Matthew McConaughey and at the Grammy Awards in February 2000 they stood shoulder-to-shoulder on the red carpet as photographers and guests alike stared agog at the green Versace creation Jennifer was wearing. (The £6,000 see-through dress barely covered her nipples and had a neckline that plunged to below her navel. The only thing that seemed to protect the singer's modesty was a single broach, placed inches away from her crotch.) Jennifer claims she did not foresee the media attention her dress would generate but the pictures that graced the pages of newspapers around the globe the following morning sent a powerful message to all the dissenters looking in on their relationship. For

CRIS JUDD

Puff and Jennifer it was business as usual – for the time being anyway.

The image of Jennifer Lopez as some gangster's moll content to stand aside, mute in the face of adversity, as her lover's freedom hangs in the balance is misguided. To say the tough Bronxite was not perturbed by the violent events of 27 December 1999 is grossly inaccurate – she had been raised in a sheltered environment and was genuinely scared on the night of the shooting. She was frightened by what her family would think when they heard the news and anxious that she would spend more than one night in the police station. She had never been in that situation before. She later told the BBC's Michael Parkinson that the arrest was a dreadful and ugly event and an experience that she never wanted to repeat, adding that she and Puff were merely in "the wrong place at the wrong time".

Despite her concerns about her brush with the law, however, her faith about Puff's innocence was never in question and the severity of the criminal charges alone did not spell the end of their union. In a 2003 interview with *Vibe* magazine she suggested that Puff's lack of commitment to the relationship was the main reason for

CRIS JUDD

its failure. Jennifer had no proof, no damning evidence, but she felt she may have been a woman wronged. Puff also admitted to VH1 that his fear of commitment had a bearing on their separation. The strain of the trial and the demands of a long-distance relationship only made the situation worse and in February 2001 the couple split. Though they would remain friends, another chapter in the love life of Jennifer Lopez had come to an end.

To onlookers it was a case of new album, new lover when rumours surfaced linking Jennifer to a back-up dancer who appeared in her latest music video. Her new single, the first from her second album *J.Lo,* fanned the flames of speculation. The sentiments expressed in the song *Love Don't Cost a Thing* seemed to provide a soundtrack to the real-life drama surrounding her, while the video appeared to be a four-minute message to Puff. It opens with Lopez, weighed down with jewellery, speaking to her lover on the phone. He cannot be with her at the moment, but in his absence he sends her expensive gifts to demonstrate his affection. Furious, she storms to the beach, stripping herself of him along the way. The cash, the car, the money, the clothes, the house, the

CRIS JUDD

flowers all mean nothing to her. Her love cannot be bought. Time, genuine affection, is free. The final scene speaks as a symbol of her emancipation and, as she wades in the sea, she thrusts her vest at the camera leaving herself naked except for a pair of panties. Anyone who did not see the significance of that video, or who failed to appreciate the happy coincidence of its timing, had to be deaf, blind and dumb or at least not distracted by the tittle-tattle of celebrity gossip.

Tucked away in the background of that video was a dancer called Cris Judd. Jennifer would not publicly admit their romance for months, but he was indeed her new love interest. If she had plucked someone off the street at random she could not have found a man more different to Puff in looks, demeanour and financial status. The producer and his love rival, the dancer and choreographer, were around the same age, both were good looking and worked in the entertainment industry, but there the common ground between the two men ended. Cristan Lee Judd was born in Texas in August 1969. Though he had toured as a dancer with Michael Jackson in the mid-Nineties his profile and wealth could not compete with that of Puff.

CRIS JUDD

Once again rumours swirled around Jennifer – first of a romance, then of an engagement. This time the murmurings were correct. By September 2001 P Diddy (as Puff Daddy now called himself) was a man free from the threat of a long-term prison sentence, but all hopes of a reconciliation with his former girlfriend were dashed when she walked down the aisle for the second time. At the end of that month, in a private ceremony in California, as the news agenda continued to be dominated by the devastating September 11th terrorist attacks, Jennifer Lopez became Mrs Cris Judd.

The marriage started off promisingly. In October 2001 the newlyweds were the guests of Donatella Versace at a party the designer threw for them in Italy. Jennifer seemed to have learned from the pitfalls of her past relationships with David Cruz and Ojani Noa – both men, who like Judd, stood in the shadow of her escalating wealth and career. Determined that her professional life would not wreck this marriage Jennifer took steps to include Cris in her business affairs. Two weeks before they were married her husband-to-be choreographed her first ever concert, which was performed in the birthplace of her parents, Puerto

CRIS JUDD

Rico. Also, while they were on honeymoon, Cris helped his wife to compose a song that would feature on the soundtrack to *Enough,* one of her upcoming movies. As Jennifer toured the world promoting her new album and her new film, *The Wedding Planner*, she assured magazine interviewers that she was in love and that finally she had found someone who cared for the real woman behind the persona. But, alas, the couple's marriage was not to last. In July 2002 Jennifer filed for divorce and, yet again, no sooner had she ended her union with one man than she was linked to another in the press.

By the age of 32 Jennifer Lopez had dated her high school sweetheart, married and divorced a waiter, enjoyed the high life with the king of bling-bling and wed one of her backing dancers. But her relationship history was not a seedy one – there were no stories of her having one-night stands with a series of anonymous men. Nevertheless, guessing whom Jennifer would date or marry next had become a daily sport in the tabloids on both sides of the Atlantic. Celebrity relationships are notoriously short-lived and often the source of public merriment but the hoopla that surrounded J-Lo had not been seen in Hollywood since the

JENNIFER LOPEZ

CRIS JUDD

Sixties and the heyday of Elizabeth Taylor. The push and pull of press speculation was something that Jennifer herself helped to feed – by falling in love so hard, so quickly, and by expressing her emotions candidly in interviews and in her work. But none of her liaisons to date would fill as many column inches as her romance with Ben Affleck.

Both of them had been there before. Ben Affleck and Jennifer Lopez were no strangers to the challenges involved when one famous person dates another. Ben had witnessed it a few years before when he stepped out with the actress Gwyneth Paltrow and the memory of her experience with P Diddy was still fresh in Jennifer's mind. If the press had thought for one minute that there was a period of overlap between Jennifer's marriage to Cris Judd and her love connection with Ben the whiff of scandal would have been especially hard to subdue. So when the two actors were linked on a personal level shortly after filming the romantic comedy *Gigli* they were quite forceful in their insistence that theirs was a professional relationship, or at least one that did not develop further until they were both free to pursue it.

11

Bennifer

BENNIFER

Y et 2002 was to be the beginning of Jennifer's romance with Affleck and by the time her divorce from husband number two was finalised in January 2003 she was already making preparations to walk down the aisle for the third time. In November, in an interview for the American network ABC, Jennifer admitted to interviewer Diane Sawyer that Ben had proposed and she had accepted. The actor had gone down on one knee in the traditional fashion and presented her with a pink diamond engagement ring rumoured to cost over $1,000,000.

As 2002 galloped into 2003 Ben Affleck and

BENNIFER

Jennifer Lopez were inseparable. Where once his name would always be connected with that of his best friend and fellow Oscar winner Matt Damon it was now placed as an adjunct to that of his fiancée. The names Ben and Jen were so often mentioned in the papers and on television celebrity reports that the press coined the tag 'Bennifer'. The couple attempted to make light of the media attention by mocking the tabloid coverage they received. In Jennifer's 2003 video *Jenny from the Block* Affleck makes a guest appearance as the glamourous sidekick of his future wife, constantly snapped by the paparazzi as they go about their daily lives. The couple are filmed taking in the sun on a yacht, lounging around in their apartment and even filling their car with gas. All the while the click of the flash bulb, the zoom of the camera lens, is never far behind.

The parody of their daily experience was accurate. It was art imitating life. For a period of time the world went Bennifer crazy, with magazines and newspapers scrutinising every aspect of the couple's time together. As Ben's style moved away from that of preppy college grad – not overtly concerned with fashion – to that of sculpted, *GQ* man complete with slicked

BENNIFER

back hair (and, when the occasion demanded it, tailored suits) an accusatory finger was pointed at Jennifer. This was her influence; her bling was rubbing off on him. It was as if the two people were morphing into one. Ken had found his Barbie and was showering her with gifts and she was showering him right back. What with the cars and the jewellery and their 83-acre Savannah, Georgia mansion (rumoured to cost them $16 million) Bennifer seemed set to become a permanent fixture on the celebrity circuit. All they had to do was walk down the aisle and they would become the next Hollywood 'it' couple. Like Jennifer Aniston and Brad Pitt, Michael Douglas and Catherine Zeta-Jones, their stars would have shone brighter just because they were together; the brilliance of the one reflecting the dazzle of the other. In July 2003, as the actors did the promotional interviews for their film *Gigli*, interviewers voiced the question on everyone's lips: "Have you set a date for the wedding?"

But, alas, it was not to be. By the autumn of 2003, as press speculation about the forthcoming nuptials reached fever pitch, the relationship crumbled. By all accounts the church had been booked and the guests had been invited, but at the last minute Jen and Ben called it off, blaming "excessive media attention". A brief break-up, then reunion, ensued before the couple finally called it quits in January 2004.

Once again Jennifer had embarked on a whirlwind romance. Once again her attempts at forging a partnership for life. When both publicity camps officially confirmed the end of the Affleck/Lopez affair, no explanation was given for the split. Rumours floated around suggesting that this or that person in each one's family disapproved of the potential marriage. Ben was said to be upset at Jennifer's excessive demands and frustrated that his wedding was becoming a lavish extravaganza. The flop of their joint project *Gigli* was also cited as a possible reason for the break-up. The critics were merciless in their response and moviegoers in America gave it an ice-cold reception by staying away in droves. For those who thought the Bennifer affair was a calculated publicity stunt, designed to drum up interest in their joint venture, the end of the engagement was a foreseeable conclusion. Both parties emphatically denied such reports.

On the contrary, for Jennifer the relationship with Ben was genuine. As with Puff and Cris she felt the two of them were destined to be together and she said as much in *Dear Ben,* a song she co-wrote as a tribute to him on her fourth album, *This is Me, Then.* To Jennifer he was 'perfect' and she was 'addicted' to his 'touch'. God created him for her and he was her dream made manifest. It was unimaginable that she would leave him. When the unimaginable happened Jennifer must have been heartbroken that yet another one of her loves had been downgraded to the position of friend.

Rifle through the romantic partnerships of Jennifer Lopez and it is easy to get confused. Everything about her Roman Catholic upbringing told her that marriage is forever – the sanctity of that union, before the eyes of God at least, secure. Yet she attached herself to husbands or potential husbands with a rapidity that was stunning. A cursory glance through her relationship history and it is easy to conclude that she succumbed to that Tinseltown affliction – an inability to love one other person for the rest of your life. On closer inspection the reality was much more grounding. She was just a person making mistakes in life, only hers were done in public.

As the press sharpened their pencils, eager to

see who J-Lo would fall for next, one single question remained. It was not the usual 'why can't X find a good man?' sort of query so often thrown up in women's magazines when a high-profile career girl fails to secure a steady relationship. It was a more fundamental one that struck at the heart of who she was and is. Who is this woman who seems to have it all but the one-on-one companionship every human being holds dear? Who is this person who, like Karen Sisco in *Out of Sight*, presents the image of a ballsy, confident broad on one hand yet bounces from failed relationship to failed relationship, on the other? In other words, who is Jennifer Lopez?

12

A global fascination

A GLOBAL FASCINATION

T he answer to that question lies in Jennifer's response to her failed trip down the aisle.

Most brides-to-be, who are forced to postpone their wedding days before they make it to the altar, are (though they might not realise it) blessed. They can take their time to assess what happened in the comfort of their own homes and behind closed doors. They can go over the facts, examine the past and peruse the days leading up to the tragedy in peace, with their families and girlfriends at hand, and a box of tissues at the ready. They can even rage against their boyfriends – in the street if they need to – and as loudly as they want – anything to rid

A GLOBAL FASCINATION

themselves of the disappointment, hurt and pain they will undoubtedly be feeling.

In September 2003 Jennifer Lopez, actress and singer, was not afforded that luxury. She was a global superstar. Her intended was Ben Affleck and their failure to make it to the church on time had been closely followed by the world. On the days that she should have been on a luxurious honeymoon, or celebrating her marriage with those closest to her, she was photographed in Miami, Florida strolling out of the sea in a bikini and stepping out of a club at night. Who was this woman who, even at an emotionally turbulent time, with cameras thrust in her face from every angle, could maintain her dignity? What was it about her that, when the rest of us would crumble and turn our face to the wall in a bid to salvage some grain of privacy, she was happy to show everyone that she was doing fine? Clearly she was someone who had guts of steel.

Leaf through Jennifer's past and it is no surprise that she reacted the way she did. Jenny from the block had come too far, worked too hard, sacrificed too much, to let a broken association with some man steal her dream. She had fought too many battles and overcome too many hurdles to run away and hide now. Like the devoted student she

A GLOBAL FASCINATION

was she had heeded the lesson her mother taught her more than a decade before. If she was to get anywhere in show business – a game where image is as important as substance – she had to toughen up. So while her skin looked smooth as she emerged, goddess-like from the sea, in reality it was as tough as a rhino's hide after a prolonged period under the African sun. This was, after all a Bronxite, the stereotypical tough New Yorker. And even if she felt devastated inside she was never going to show it to the world on the outside.

It is this brashness of Jennifer – this cocky-in-your-face side to her personality – that has often got her into trouble. It is the reason why she is loved and hated in equal measure. Pick any person aged between six and 60 on the streets of the Western world, ask them if they like J-Lo and watch their response. First of all, for most of them, the brand recognition would be immediate, as it would be if you had mentioned Coca-Cola or McDonald's. And secondly, while some of them would profess to be disinterested in such matters, a sizeable proportion would say she is fantastic and an equally large group would say they loathe her. There is no in-between, no middle ground, she provokes a strong reaction.

JENNIFER LOPEZ

A GLOBAL FASCINATION

And why should this be? Here is a woman who has a remarkable success story. She is the good Catholic girl, the all-round student who went against her parents' wishes and followed her dreams. Hers is the story of hard graft. She didn't descend from a Hollywood dynasty – another link in the chain, another cardboard cut-out who could pick a good script the moment she came out of her mother's womb. Instead she had nearly everything going against, not least her race. The only thing she had going for her was her determination and her talent.

Nearly two decades later she has achieved a formidable array of 'firsts'. She was the first Hispanic actress to be paid $1 million for a title role in a movie. She was the first Latina to receive a major cosmetics contract when, following the success of *Selena* and *Out of Sight*, she became the global face of L'Oreal. And she continues to tear down walls. Now Jennifer Lopez, or J-Lo, is a viable brand, a lifestyle and image that can be bought and sold much like any other. Not only is she a dancer, actress and singer, she is the figurehead of her own empire. She has fulfilled the promise of Selena Quintanilla Perez and mirrored the achievements of Sean 'P Diddy' Coombs by launching her own range of clothes, her own perfume (Glow) and her own restaurant (Madre's in Los Angeles). From her humble beginnings in Castle Hill, the Bronx, Jennifer Lopez has become a multi-millionaire and, it would seem, a female heroine and a minority-ethnic champion along the way.

Yet in the daily reports of the minute details of this woman's life few of these positive aspects are mentioned. Instead what rages around her is controversy and she seems forever destined to be accused of being the opposite of what she seeks to portray. In her music, for example, she has always aimed to connect with her urban roots. Right from the very beginning of her singing career, with *On the 6*, Jennifer sought to capture all the elements of her personality and heritage. It had a little bit of hip-hop, a pinch of R&B, a dash of dance, a heaped tablespoon of pop and a generous helping of Latin-soul. Her videos too were designed to appeal to her multi-ethnic audience. The storyboard for *I'm Gonna Be Alright* (a song she performed with the rapper Nas) showed her doing normal things in the 'hood'. Here's a shot of Jennifer with rollers in her hair. Here's another one of her washing her clothes in the laundrette and one more of her enjoying a summer's day by playing softball with the guys on the block.

Although she has always been proud of her roots, when the lyrics on the remix version of the single *I'm Real*, came under the spotlight, she was accused of being a racist. Even though other Latino hip-hop artists freely used the term many in the black community felt she had overstepped the mark. Her old flame, P Diddy, defended her by insisting she was not a racist. In the end Jennifer came out fighting on her own behalf saying any suggestion that she was prejudiced was 'hurtful' and 'absurd'.

To be Jennifer, it seems, is to be someone who is forever misunderstood and nothing could be more misunderstood than her image. The public persona of J-Lo is of a woman with a larger than life attitude. She is – if press reports are to be believed – the diva of all divas. Television executives, beware, we are told. Invite this woman on one of your shows and you could wallpaper a small house with her demands. The claims are now part of pop culture – the insistence on all-white dressing rooms, bottled water at a certain temperature and tea stirred in a specific direction. Then there's the entourage, so big it could populate a small island.

JENNIFER LOPEZ

A GLOBAL FASCINATION

Her professionalism, her determination to get things right and to set high standards for herself and those around her, are constantly misread, misinterpreted as inflated self-importance.

Jennifer's response to these reports is always the same. She dismisses them. And, when all else fails, she laughs them off. In November 2001 when she went to collect a Top of the Pops Artist on Top of the World award she mocked tabloid reports that she was a 'demanding diva' by thanking, her entourage – her two chefs, masseuse, 20 bodyguards, three assistants, four band members, six dancers and two handmaidens. Her tongue was lodged firmly in her cheek the whole time.

Jennifer's sense of humour about her tabloid image was nothing new. Back in February 2001, when she hosted (and performed on) America's long-running sketch-comedy show, *Saturday Night Live*, she was happy to poke fun at her most-talked about asset – her bottom; the same one that was supposedly insured for $1billion. J-Lo, it seemed, had the grace to laugh at herself.

And well she might. You see, despite all the criticism that is levelled against her, Jennifer Lopez is a success. Mistake her confidence for arrogance. Dismiss her quest for perfectionism as the actions of

A GLOBAL FASCINATION

a diva. Do all those things at will and you fall into the realm of (to borrow a hip-hop term) 'haters'. But do that and you miss the point. Because, love her or loathe her, the crucial fact is you cannot ignore Jennifer Lopez. As she took the stage to perform *Play* that night on *SNL* in 2001 Jennifer must have appreciated that last point. She must have known that, in the end, she had won, she had answered her critics. Standing in the very city where her story began, with a number one movie and hit song under her belt, performing live before the nation, she must have felt a tingle of satisfaction. She had done it.

There is nothing more exhilarating for a human being than to realise their dream. To fulfil their life's purpose. Scattered around the world are people who, as children, painted wild, glorious futures for themselves. Countless kids have wanted to be rock stars, screen idols and dancers. Neighbourhoods are littered with future astronauts and rocket scientists, even firemen and cops. But somewhere along the line, on their road to adulthood, life gets in the way and sucks all the colour and imagination out of their existence, leaving something arid in its wake. And so the next Jean Harlow becomes an office clerk and the man who wanted to become Elvis, as the song suggests,

A GLOBAL FASCINATION

works in a chip shop. That was not the case with Jennifer Lopez. She carried those childhood dreams; she watered them, fed them and willed them to grow.

She set out to be a dancer and, as a Fly Girl, she became one of the most recognisable movers in the country. She said she wanted to be an actress and she won some of the most coveted roles in Hollywood, collecting awards and nominations along the way. She revealed a passion for singing, only to knock out hit album after hit album. Everything she set out to do, she has done. She is a powerful, fearless person.

And that is why Jennifer Lopez provokes derision and applause wherever her name is mentioned. It is because of who she is. Her very essence has the ability to inspire some, to repel others. Her story speaks to millions of young people around the world, because it is the American dream personified; the idea that that nation was founded upon. No matter who you are, where you come from or how much money you have, you can do anything you put your mind to. The single, greatest turn-off/turn-on (delete where applicable) about J-Lo is this: like other great achievers, the mere existence of a Jennifer Lopez suggests to the rest of us that we

A GLOBAL FASCINATION

could be better, if we really tried.

In the end, the little girl from Castle Hill got what she wanted. The movies, the fame, the cash, the clothes, the jewellery, the adoration, the glamour, the glitz they are all hers for the taking. And, as the world continues to turn, so does the global fascination with Jennifer Lopez. Post-Bennifer, five years after the New York shooting with Puff, with a second husband sandwiched in between, the love life of ` is still tabloid fodder. This time the finger of suspicion points to Marc Anthony – the Latin singer who leant his vocals to her debut album. His marriage to his wife crumbled just as Bennifer was laid to rest. The two have been spotted in each other's company and, hey presto, the merry-go-round has begun again. The incessant clatter of the rumour mill is never-ending and the louder it gets the more it threatens to drown out what is important.

It's a shame really, because amid the tabloid tittle-tattle, lost among the sea of paparazzi shots, is a news headline worthy of recognition. In April 2004 Jennifer Lopez followed in the footsteps of Martin Scorsese, Robert De Niro, Jack Lemmon and Jessica Lange by appearing on Inside the Actor's Studio. The television show is an interview

A GLOBAL FASCINATION

and thorough examination of an artist's work, filmed at the prestigious drama school, The Actors Studio in New York, where greats like Paul Newman and Al Pacino once learnt their craft. As she took her seat before the host James Lipton, Jennifer Lopez became the first Latina to be interviewed on the programme. It was quite an achievement and another worthy addition to her CV. It was a sign that she was respected within the acting community and that was no small feat. Because, despite what anyone says about her, Jennifer's success in Hollywood has been achieved on her own terms. She is one of the most celebrated Latin-American actresses of all time and she has reached that lofty position without changing her name like Rita Hayworth or wearing a pile of fruit on her head like Carmen Miranda. She has paved a way and carved a road, making it slightly easier for the Hispanic performers who come after her.

The impact Jennifer has had on Hollywood is similar to that of Halle Berry who, in 2002 became the first African-American to win an Academy Award for her performance as an actress in a lead role. Their existence has not changed the town overnight, but their determination to be defined by their ability and not by their colour has encouraged

A GLOBAL FASCINATION

casting directors to think just a smidgen outside the box. From now on when a young Latino actress arrives in the town, with a pocket-full of dreams, she can do so confident that a woman has gone before her and opened the door that little bit further.

And that, not the cars, not the money, not the songs and certainly not the men, is the greatest achievement of Jennifer Lynn Lopez.

13

Filmography

JENNIFER LOPEZ

FILMOGRAPHY

My Little Girl (1986)

My Family, Mi Familia (1995)

Money Train (1995)

Jack (1996)

Blood and Wine (1997)

Selena (1997)

Anaconda (1997)

U Turn (1997)

Out of Sight (1998)

Antz (1998)

The Cell (2000)

The Wedding Planner (2001)

Angel Eyes (2001)

Enough (2002)

Maid in Manhattan (2003)

Gigli (2003)

Jersey Girl (2004)

14

Discography

JENNIFER LOPEZ

DISCOGRAPHY

Album – *On the 6*
Singles
If You Had My Love
Waitin' For Tonight
Feeling So Good

Album – *J.Lo*
Singles
Love Don't Cost A thing
I'm Real
Play
Ain't It Funny
I'm Gonna Be Alright

J to Tha L-o! The Remixes
Singles
I'm Real (Murder remix featuring Ja Rule)
Ain't it Funny (Murder remix featuring Ja Rule)

Album – *This is Me, Then*
Singles
Jenny from the Block (featuring Styles and Jadakiss)
I'm Glad
All I Have (featuring LL Cool J)
Baby I Love U!

BIOGRAPHIES

OTHER BOOKS IN THE SERIES

Also available in the series:

OTHER BOOKS IN THE SERIES

JENNIFER ANISTON

She's been a Friend to countless millions worldwide, and overcame numerous hurdles to rise to the very top of her field. From a shy girl with a dream of being a famous actress, through being reduced to painting scenery for high school plays, appearing in a series of flop TV shows and one rather bad movie, Jennifer Aniston has persevered, finally finding success at the very top of the TV tree.

Bringing the same determination that got her a part on the world's best-loved TV series to her attempts at a film career, she's also worked her way from rom-com cutie up to serious, respected actress and box office draw, intelligently combining indie, cult and comedy movies into a blossoming career which looks set to shoot her to the heights of Hollywood's A-list. She's also found love with one of the world's most desirable men. Is Jennifer Aniston the ultimate Hollywood Renaissance woman? It would seem she's got more than a shot at such a title, as indeed, she seems to have it all, even if things weren't always that way. Learn all about Aniston's rise to fame in this compelling biography.

OTHER BOOKS IN THE SERIES

DAVID BECKHAM

This book covers the amazing life of the boy from East London who has not only become a world class footballer and the captain of England, but also an idol to millions, and probably the most famous man in Britain.

His biography tracks his journey, from the playing fields of Chingford to the Bernabau. It examines how he joined his beloved Manchester United and became part of a golden generation of talent that led to United winning trophies galore.

Beckham's parallel personal life is also examined, as he moved from tongue-tied football-obsessed kid to suitor of a Spice Girl, to one half of Posh & Becks, the most famous celebrity couple in Britain – perhaps the world. His non-footballing activities, his personal indulgences and changing styles have invited criticism, and even abuse, but his football talent has confounded the critics, again and again.

The biography looks at his rise to fame and his relationship with Posh, as well as his decision to leave Manchester for Madrid. Has it affected his relationship with Posh? What will the latest controversy over his sex life mean for celebrity's royal couple? And will he come back to play in England again?

OTHER BOOKS IN THE SERIES

GEORGE CLOONEY

The tale of George Clooney's astonishing career is an epic every bit as riveting as one of his blockbuster movies. It's a story of tenacity and determination, of fame and infamy, a story of succeeding on your own terms regardless of the risks. It's also a story of emergency rooms, batsuits, tidal waves and killer tomatoes, but let's not get ahead of ourselves.

Born into a family that, by Sixties' Kentucky standards, was dripping with show business glamour, George grew up seeing the hard work and heartache that accompanied a life in the media spotlight.

By the time stardom came knocking for George Clooney, it found a level-headed and mature actor ready and willing to embrace the limelight, while still indulging a lifelong love of partying and practical jokes. A staunchly loyal friend and son, a bachelor with a taste for the high life, a vocal activist for the things he believes and a born and bred gentleman; through failed sitcoms and blockbuster disasters, through artistic credibility and box office success, George Clooney has remained all of these things...and much, much more. Prepare to meet Hollywood's most fascinating megastar in this riveting biography.

OTHER BOOKS IN THE SERIES

BILLY CONNOLLY

In a 2003 London Comedy Poll to find Britain's favourite comedian, Billy Connolly came out on top. It's more than just Billy Connolly's all-round comic genius that puts him head and shoulders above the rest. Connolly has also proved himself to be an accomplished actor with dozens of small and big screen roles to his name. In 2003, he could be seen in *The Last Samurai* with Tom Cruise.

Connolly has also cut the mustard in the USA, 'breaking' that market in a way that chart-topping pop groups since The Beatles and the Stones have invariably failed to do, let alone mere stand-up comedians. Of course, like The Beatles and the Stones, Billy Connolly has been to the top of the pop charts too with D.I.V.O.R.C.E. in 1975.

On the way he's experienced heartache of his own with a difficult childhood and a divorce of his own, found the time and energy to bring up five children, been hounded by the press on more than one occasion, and faced up to some considerable inner demons. But Billy Connolly is a survivor. Now in his 60s, he's been in show business for all of 40 years, and 2004 finds him still touring. This exciting biography tells the story an extraordinary entertainer.

OTHER BOOKS IN THE SERIES

ROBERT DE NIRO

Robert De Niro is cinema's greatest chameleon. Snarling one minute, smirking the next, he's straddled Hollywood for a quarter of a century, making his name as a serious character actor, in roles ranging from psychotic taxi drivers to hardened mobsters. The scowls and pent-up violence may have won De Niro early acclaim but, ingeniously, he's now playing them for laughs, poking fun at the tough guy image he so carefully cultivated. Ever the perfectionist, De Niro holds nothing back on screen, but in real life he is a very private man – he thinks of himself as just another guy doing a job. Some job, some guy. There's more to the man than just movies. De Niro helped New York pick itself up after the September 11 terrorist attacks on the Twin Towers by launching the TriBeCa Film Festival and inviting everyone downtown. He runs several top-class restaurants and has dated some of the most beautiful women in the world, least of all supermodel Naomi Campbell. Now in his 60s, showered with awards and a living legend, De Niro's still got his foot on the pedal. There are six, yes six, films coming your way in 2004. In this latest biography, you'll discover all about his latest roles and the life of this extraordinary man.

OTHER BOOKS IN THE SERIES

MICHAEL DOUGLAS

Douglas may have been a shaggy-haired member of a hippy commune in the Sixties but just like all the best laidback, free-loving beatniks, he's gone on to blaze a formidable career, in both acting and producing.

In a career that has spanned nearly 40 years so far, Douglas has produced a multitude of hit movies including the classic *One Flew Over The Cuckoo's Nest* and *The China Syndrome* through to box office smashes such as *Starman* and *Face/Off*.

His acting career has been equally successful – from *Romancing The Stone* to *Wall Street* to *Fatal Attraction*, Douglas's roles have shown that he isn't afraid of putting himself on the line when up there on the big screen.

His relationship with his father; his stay in a top clinic to combat his drinking problem; the breakdown of his first marriage; and his publicised clash with the British media have all compounded to create the image of a man who's transformed himself from being the son of Hollywood legend Kirk Douglas, into Kirk Douglas being the dad of Hollywood legend, Michael Douglas.

OTHER BOOKS IN THE SERIES

HUGH GRANT

He's the Oxford fellow who stumbled into acting, the middle-class son of a carpet salesman who became famous for bumbling around stately homes and posh weddings. The megastar actor who claims he doesn't like acting, but has appeared in over 40 movies and TV shows.

On screen he's romanced a glittering array of Hollywood's hottest actresses, and tackled medical conspiracies and the mafia. Off screen he's hogged the headlines with his high profile girlfriend as well as finding lifelong notoriety after a little Divine intervention in Los Angeles.

Hugh Grant is Britain's biggest movie star, an actor whose talent for comedy has often been misjudged by those who assume he simply plays himself.

From bit parts in Nottingham theatre, through comedy revues at the Edinburgh Fringe, and on to the top of the box office charts, Hugh has remained constant – charming, witty and ever so slightly sarcastic, obsessed with perfection and performance while winking to his audience as if to say: "This is all awfully silly, isn't it?" Don't miss this riveting biography.

OTHER BOOKS IN THE SERIES

MICHAEL JACKSON

Friday 29 August 1958 was not a special day in Gary, Indiana, and indeed Gary, was far from being a special place. But it was on this day and in this location that the world's greatest entertainer was to be born, Michael Joseph Jackson.

The impact that this boy was destined to have on the world of entertainment could never have been estimated. Here we celebrate Michael Jackson's extraordinary talents, and plot the defining events over his 40-year career. This biography explores the man behind the myth, and gives an understanding of what drives this special entertainer.

In 1993, there was an event that was to rock Jackson's world. His friendship with a 12-year-old boy and the subsequent allegations resulted in a lawsuit, a fall in record sales and a long road to recovery. Two marriages, three children and 10 years later there is a feeling of déjà vu as Jackson again deals with more controversy. Without doubt, 2004 proves to be the most important year in the singer's life. Whatever that future holds for Jackson, his past is secured, there has never been and there will never again be anything quite like Michael Jackson.

OTHER BOOKS IN THE SERIES

NICOLE KIDMAN

On 23 March 2003 Nicole Kidman won the Oscar for Best Actress for her role as Virginia Woolf in *The Hours*. That was the night that marked Nicole Kidman's acceptance into the upper echelons of Hollywood royalty. She had certainly come a long way from the 'girlfriend' roles she played when she first arrived in Hollywood – in films such as *Billy Bathgate* and *Batman Forever* – although even then she managed to inject her 'pretty girl' roles with an edge that made her acting stand out. And she was never merely content to be Mrs Cruise, movie star's wife. Although she stood dutifully behind her then husband in 1993 when he was given his star on the Hollywood Walk of Fame, Nicole got a star of her own 10 years later, in 2003.

Not only does Nicole Kidman have stunning good looks and great pulling power at the box office, she also has artistic credibility. But Nicole has earned the respect of her colleagues, working hard and turning in moving performances from a very early age. Although she dropped out of school at 16, no one doubts the intelligence and passion that are behind the fiery redhead's acting career, which includes television and stage work, as well as films. Find out how Kidman became one of Hollywood's most respected actresses in this compelling biography.

OTHER BOOKS IN THE SERIES

MADONNA

Everyone thought they had Madonna figured out in early 2003. The former Material Girl had become Maternal Girl, giving up on causing controversy to look after her two children and set up home in England with husband Guy Ritchie. The former wild child had settled down and become respectable. The new Madonna would not do anything to shock the establishment anymore, she'd never do something like snogging both Britney Spears and Christina Aguilera at the MTV Video Music Awards... or would she?

Of course she would. Madonna has been constantly reinventing herself since she was a child, and her ability to shock even those who think they know better is both a tribute to her business skills and the reason behind her staying power. Only Madonna could create gossip with two of the current crop of pop princesses in August and then launch a children's book in September. In fact, only Madonna would even try.

In her 20-year career she has not just been a successful pop singer, she is also a movie star, a business woman, a stage actress, an author and a mother. Find out all about this extraordinary modern-day icon in this new compelling biography.

OTHER BOOKS IN THE SERIES

BRAD PITT

From the launch pad that was his scene stealing turn in *Thelma And Louise* as the sexual-enlightening bad boy. To his character-driven performances in dramas such as *Legends of the Fall* through to his Oscar-nominated work in *Twelve Monkeys* and the dark and razor-edged Tyler Durden in *Fight Club*, Pitt has never rested on his laurels. Or his good looks.

And the fact that his love life has garnered headlines all over the world hasn't hindered Brad Pitt's profile away from the screen either – linked by the press to many women, his relationships with the likes of Juliette Lewis and Gwyneth Paltrow. Then of course, in 2000, we had the Hollywood fairytale ending when he tied the silk knot with Jennifer Aniston.

Pitt's impressive track record as a superstar, sex symbol *and* credible actor looks set to continue as he has three films lined up for release over the next year – as Achilles in the Wolfgang Peterson-helmed Troy; Rusty Ryan in the sequel *Ocean's Twelve* and the titular Mr Smith in the thriller *Mr & Mrs Smith* alongside Angelina Jolie. Pitt's ever-growing success shows no signs of abating. Discover all about Pitt's meteoric rise from rags to riches in this riveting biography.

OTHER BOOKS IN THE SERIES

SHANE RICHIE

Few would begrudge the current success of 40-year-old Shane Richie. To get where he is today, Shane has had a rather bumpy roller coaster ride that has seen the hard working son of poor Irish immigrants endure more than his fair share of highs and lows – financially, professionally and personally.

In the space of four decades he has amused audiences at school plays, realised his childhood dream of becoming a Pontins holiday camp entertainer, experienced homelessness, beat his battle with drink, became a millionaire then lost the lot. He's worked hard and played hard.

When the producers of *EastEnders* auditioned Shane for a role in the top TV soap, they decided not to give him the part, but to create a new character especially for him. That character was Alfie Moon, manager of the Queen Vic pub, and very quickly Shane's TV alter ego has become one of the most popular soap characters in Britain. This biography is the story of a boy who had big dreams and never gave up on turning those dreams into reality

OTHER BOOKS IN THE SERIES

JONNY WILKINSON

"There's 35 seconds to go, this is the one. It's coming back for Jonny Wilkinson. He drops for World Cup glory. It's over! He's done it! Jonny Wilkinson is England's Hero yet again..."

That memorable winning drop kick united the nation, and lead to the start of unprecedented victory celebrations throughout the land. In the split seconds it took for the ball to leave his boot and slip through the posts, Wilkinson's life was to change forever. It wasn't until three days later, when the squad flew back to Heathrow and were met with a rapturous reception, that the enormity of their win, began to sink in.

Like most overnight success stories, Wilkinson's journey has been a long and dedicated one. He spent 16 years 'in rehearsal' before achieving his finest performance, in front of a global audience of 22 million, on that rainy evening in Telstra Stadium, Sydney.

But how did this modest self-effacing 24-year-old become England's new number one son? This biography follows Jonny's journey to international stardom. Find out how he caught the rugby bug, what and who his earliest influences were and what the future holds for our latest English sporting hero.

OTHER BOOKS IN THE SERIES

ROBBIE WILLIAMS

Professionally, things can't get much better for Robbie Williams. In 2002 he signed the largest record deal in UK history when he re-signed with EMI. The following year he performed to over 1.5 million fans on his European tour, breaking all attendance records at Knebworth with three consecutive sell-out gigs.

Since going solo Robbie Williams has achieved five number one hit singles, five number one hit albums; 10 Brits and three Ivor Novello awards. When he left the highly successful boy band Take That in 1995 his future seemed far from rosy. He got off to a shaky start. His nemesis, Gary Barlow, had already recorded two number one singles and the press had virtually written Williams off. But then in December 1997, he released his Christmas single, *Angels.*

Angels re-launched his career – it remained in the Top 10 for 11 weeks. Since then Robbie has gone from strength to strength, both as a singer and a natural showman. His live videos are a testament to his performing talent and his promotional videos are works of art.

This biography tells of Williams' journey to the top – stopping off on the way to take a look at his songs, his videos, his shows, his relationships, his rows, his record deals and his demons.